Paul Kirk's Championship
Barbecue Sauces

Paul Kirk's Championship Barbecue Sauces

175 Make-Your-Own Sauces, Marinades, Dry Rubs, Wet Rubs, Mops, and Salsas

Paul Kirk

The Harvard Common Press
Boston, Massachusetts

The Harvard Common Press
535 Albany Street
Boston, Massachusetts 02118

Printed in the United States of America
Printed on acid-free paper

Library of Congress Cataloging-in-Publication Data
Kirk, Paul.
    Paul Kirk's championship barbecue sauces : 175 make-your-own
sauces, marinades, dry rubs, wet rubs, mops, and salsas / Paul Kirk.
        p.   cm.
    Includes index.
    ISBN 1-55832-124-1 (alk. paper).—ISBN 1-55832-125-X
(pbk.: alk. paper)
        1. Barbecue cookery. 2. Barbecue sauce. 3. Marinades.
4. Cookery (Salsas) I. Title
    TX840.B3K454   1997
    641.5'784--dc21   97-6626

Cover and text design by Joyce C. Weston
Cover photographs by Kimberly Grant
Illustrations by Chris Van Dusen

10 9 8 7 6 5

For Jessica, Todd, Chrissy, and Erin

Contents

Acknowledgments

I want to thank my mother and father for my love and appreciation of good food. Thanks to my wife, Jessica, and my children, Todd, Chrissy, and Erin, my biggest fans. Thanks also to the rest of my family, Mary Beth, Cathy, Tom, Marty, Jenny, and Joyce, for all of their encouragement. I would like to acknowledge the barbecue public for its quest for greater and greater barbecue, and for living up to the Backyard Barbecue Creed, "Always Strive to Make Your Barbecue Better." And, finally, I want to thank the one who is most responsible for getting this cookbook written and published, my patron saint, St. Jude—the Saint of the Impossible!

Introduction

There's a Peace Corps motto that goes "Feed a man a fish and feed him for a day. Teach a man how to fish and feed him for life." My motto is "If you give people barbecue, they will eat and enjoy it once. Teach people to barbecue, they will eat and enjoy barbecue for the rest of their lives." So this is a book that tells you what I think you need to know about barbecue. Better yet, it's a barbecue cookbook!

This book is a collection of recipes developed over fifteen years of competition barbecue and five years of The Baron's School of Pitmasters, which I have conducted all over the country. Some of the secrets I reveal here are the same ones that helped me win seven world barbecue championships. They've also helped my students go on to win thirty-five state barbecue championships and three world barbecue championships.

Knowledge of barbecue is like a man and his money: The more he learns about barbecue, the more he craves it!

This book is a guide for beginners to help them develop their own barbecue. The barbecuers who "know it all" can still get a good deal of enjoyment from this book. As the famous barbecuer William Shakespeare once said, "Doubt is called the beacon of the wise." So when I tell you to use this book as a starting point and not as gospel, you will know what I mean.

If you already have your barbecue pit set up and you know about lighting fires and all the rest of Barbecue 101, then you can skip ahead to whatever recipe chapter you want. Don't feel you have to keep reading. But if you're the kind of person who likes to take things one step at a time, here's the basic information for getting started with barbecue.

Equipment

When I barbecue, I do far more indirect cooking than I do grilling, meaning the meat is cooked slowly by smoke over a fire

Some 85 percent of all American households own one or more type of barbecue cooker. Of that 85 percent, 65 percent own a charcoal grill and 54 percent own a grill fueled by gas.

that has burned down to coals. The meat sits over a drip pan, not directly above the coals, to prevent flare-ups from fat dripping onto the fire. Most cookers can be set up for this style of cooking, such as a pit or barrel barbecue, a kettle grill, or a smoker. (For sources, see Resources.)

A water smoker is a tall, cylindrical oven that looks like a silo. You burn charcoal and wood in the bottom and a water pan sits above the coals. The food sits on a grate over the water pan and cooks in a combination of smoke and steam, or heat and moisture. You get good smoke flavor from water smokers, and the food is almost always moist and tender. As for pit smokers, there are a lot of different styles and models available, but they all have the same basic features. A firebox that handles wood chips, chunks, or logs is offset from the cooking area, which is basically a smoke chamber. Some pits have water chambers, which help to keep the meat moist. Before you invest in any pit, shop around. Consider prices, and the quality and gauge of the metal.

The most common type of barbecue is probably the kettle grill. Most people burn only charcoal in a kettle grill, but you can burn a combination of charcoal, wood chips, and wood chunks. You can get the same strong wood-smoke flavor from a kettle grill as you can from a log-burning pit. To barbecue in a kettle grill, you light the charcoal and let the coals burn down to a gray ash color. Then you push the charcoal to one side and place a drip pan filled with water on the other side. Place a handful or two of well-soaked wood chips or chunks on the coals, and set your food on the grate above the water pan or to the side of the hot coals. The food can be placed anywhere on the grate, so long as it is not above the coals. Then close the lid and cook. It helps to position a thermometer in one of the exhaust vents so you can monitor the cooking temperature. Meats are cooked at temperatures between 230 and 250°F. I recommend that you keep the temperature inside your pit, smoker, or grill within this range for any type of meat you are cooking. Only the cooking time should vary for different types of meat.

As far as gas and electric grills go, I have a lot of fun at the expense of their owners. Someone in my class will say, "I have a gas or electric grill," and I grab for my heart just like Redd Foxx did and say, "Elizabeth, it's the big one." But in reality, if I had a gas or electric grill at home, I would use it for grilling. Don't tell anybody (it might ruin my image), but I have used both and I like them. For grilling, that is, not for smoking.

Since most of the rubs and barbecue seasonings that I use have sugar in them, they can caramelize if they get too hot. You can still use them when cooking over hot coals or on a gas or electric grill, though, by making two adjustments: lowering your cooking temperature a little, and turning the meat more frequently. For example, if you usually cook the meat over medium-high heat and turn it at 20-minute intervals, then lower the heat to medium and turn it every 12 to 15 minutes.

If someone says that you're not doing real barbecue if you are charcoal grilling or using a gas or electric grill, just thank him or her for the opinion and go right on enjoying your barbecue. What that person doesn't realize is that you like the barbecue you serve. Your family and friends think it's the best barbecue since time began, and you know that it is!

Fuels

It stands to reason that if whatever you're barbecuing is cooked by the heat of the charcoal and the flavor of the smoke, the kind of smoke you are generating is going to make a difference in the taste of the meat. Personally, I like to smoke with oak and apple wood. Both oak and apple have a fruity and subtle flavor, with apple being the more exotic of the two. Some barbecuers just swear by oak. Cherry, hard maple, pecan, hickory, and mesquite are all good, flavorful woods, but their smoke will darken the meat if you overuse it. Alder is another good wood to use, if you can get it.

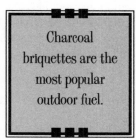

Charcoal briquettes are the most popular outdoor fuel.

You'll read that hickory is the best wood for pork and that apple and cherry are better for poultry and fish.

It's like matching food and wine. Some people just have to follow the rules, and some people will go with whatever they like. I say whatever tastes right to you and you can lay your hands on is what you should use.

Green hardwood burns hotter, longer, and smokier than does aged

> Wood chips should be soaked in water for at least a half hour before you throw them on hot coals. Sprigs of dried herbs, like rosemary, can be treated the same way.

wood in the barbecue. I like to use aged wood that has been cut and dried for at least six months.

A lot of people use hardwood chips for smoke flavor when they are cooking over charcoal or gas. You soak the chips for 30 minutes, then wrap them in heavy-duty aluminum foil, making a packet and sealing all of the seams. Punch holes in the top to let out the smoke. If you are using a gas or electric grill, place the packet of chips on the lava rocks just before you put the meat on the grill. If you are using charcoal, place it right on the hot coals. If you are cooking indirectly, add more chips every hour to hour and a half. If you are going to barbecue for a long period of time, plan out when you are going to put the chips on—at the beginning, middle, and end of the cooking time. If you think you need more smoke, plan to put chips on about four times. Remember that too little smoke is much better than too much smoke.

If you want to burn charcoal, you should try out a few different brands before settling on your house brand. Briquettes are theoretically made from sawdust burned without oxygen. In truth, you will find that charcoal can have a lot of additives—to make it burn faster, burn slower, light better, you name it. Some briquettes even have pieces of hardwood bound into them. True lump hardwood charcoal, another option, burns cleaner and lights more easily than briquettes. But it also burns hotter, so you will want to use fewer coals, and spread them out a bit more.

Fire Tending

If you use a petrochemical fire starter, use it sparingly. You don't need to flood the charcoal for it to work. This is one place where patience really helps. If you do flood the charcoal, that's about all you'll taste on your barbecue. To start the fire, you can use kindling, electric starters, propane, blow torches, whatever suits you. Let the fire burn down to white ash before you even think about starting to barbecue. The coals should be coated with ash so you can't even see any red glow. Hold your hand about 5 inches above the coals. If you can't keep your hand there for at least 5 seconds, the fire is ready.

You can't just put the food on the grill and walk away for a couple of hours and count on everything cooking just right. You have to keep and maintain the right temperature in the pit or grill. To do this, you need to learn how to control your pit or grill and take into account the weather outside (hot, cold, windy, etc.) and the size of meat you are barbecuing. Remember, every time you lift the lid on your barbecue to check on the food, you are losing heat, so you have to add to the cooking time.

You'll want a thermometer (a candy/deep fat thermometer works well) to help you keep track of the temperature in the barbecue. Then you can regulate the temperature by opening and closing vents. An instant-read thermometer will help you monitor the temperature of the meat. This is especially important when you are grilling the meat quickly, as opposed to slow-cooking it for hours.

The Basic Technique of Barbecuing

As I mentioned, and as the name of this book will tell you, my barbecue tips and secrets come from years of experience in competition barbecue. So when I think of basic barbecue techniques, there are three main cuts of meat that come to mind:

An easy way to clean a food-encrusted barbecue grill is to start your fire, let it get hot, and spread out the coals. Cover the grill grate with heavy-duty aluminum foil. Put it back on the grill over the hot coals. Let it cook for about 15 minutes. Remove the foil with tongs. Tap the grate with a spatula or brush it with a wire brush. All of the debris will come right off.

pork ribs, pork shoulders, and brisket. This isn't to say you can't barbecue chicken or whole fish or even potatoes for that matter. As I said, I love all types of grilling, and this book is filled with recipes to use on all kinds of food. But if you want to consider yourself a barbecuer as serious as the best, you need to know how to barbecue pork ribs, pork shoulders, and brisket. I outline these methods here.

> When using a meat thermometer, make sure the end of the probe is not in a pocket of fat or touching a bone.

You'll notice I've also included instructions for cooking in the oven. Well, what if a hurricane hits and you can't get the barbecue going? You can still enjoy the sauce.

Pork Ribs

Spareribs come from the belly of the pig. A tough cut, these ribs require long, slow cooking. Loin or baby back ribs are shorter than spareribs, meatier, and generally more expensive. Country-style ribs are the shoulder end of a bone-in pork loin.

When using a dry rub, you can season the ribs and let them stand for 8 hours or overnight, covered, in the refrigerator before barbecuing. I have had better success sprinkling on the rub just as you would heavily season meat with salt and pepper, and then putting the ribs on the pit right away.

Ribs are done when you can gently pull them apart with your gloved hand.

Covered grill method: Place the charcoal on one half of the lower grate, and place a disposable aluminum pan (available at most grocery stores) on the other half. Start with 2 to 2½ pounds of charcoal. Put soaked wood chips in the foil pan, and place the ribs on the upper grate, away from the fire and over the pan. Cover the grill, and cook for 4 to 8 hours, at a temperature between 230 and 250°F, adding more wood chips after half an hour. Turn the ribs about halfway through the total cooking time, and start basting them at the same time that you turn them.

Remove the ribs, and let them rest at least 15 minutes. Then cut and serve them.

Smoker method: Cook the ribs for 4 to 8 hours, at a temperature between 230 and 250°F, turning them halfway through the total cooking time. Start basting the ribs at the same time that you turn them.

Remove the ribs, and let them rest at least 15 minutes. Then cut and serve them.

For either method: Brush with your finishing sauce during the last 30 minutes of the cooking process. When I glaze with a finishing or dipping sauce, I use a pastry brush and paint the bone side of the ribs first, then turn them over and paint them on the meat side, then cover them, and cook another 10 to 15 minutes. I paint them again on the meat side one more time and finish cooking the ribs for another 10 to 15 minutes.

In the oven: Season the ribs and roast them on a rack in a roasting pan at 300°F for 3 to 4 hours. Brush with finishing sauce about 30 minutes before the ribs will be done.

Pork Shoulder

This is the cut to buy when you want to make pulled pork. After barbecuing the meat, let it sit for about 15 minutes, or until it is cool enough to handle. Then pull off chunks of meat and shred or chop it. Serve it on buns with sauce. Top with coleslaw if you want it Carolina-style, or what is called a pig sandwich.

Usually the pork shoulder is cut into two big roasts: the Boston butt and the picnic, weighing about 3 to 8 pounds each. The butt has the least amount of bone.

Covered grill method: Place the charcoal on one half of the lower grate, and place a disposable aluminum pan (available at most grocery stores) on the other half.

Start with 2 to 2½ pounds of charcoal. Put soaked wood chips in the foil pan, and place the pork shoulder on the upper grate, away from the fire and over the pan. Cover the grill, and cook the meat at a temperature between 230 and 250°F, for 1½ hours per pound or until its internal temperature reaches 170 to 180°F. Add more wood chips after half an hour. Turn the meat about

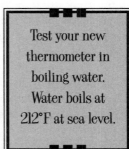

Test your new thermometer in boiling water. Water boils at 212°F at sea level.

Barbecue vs. Grilling

If someone says to me they're going to have a barbecue and cook hamburgers on the grill, I say, "Fine. Whatever." To most of us, though, barbecue means slow-cooking meat in smoke. Grilling is what you do to hamburgers—a hot fire cooks the meat quickly, searing the outside and leaving the inside still juicy.

I'm not opposed to grilling in any shape or form. You can use all the marinades, rubs, bastes, sauces, and salsas you find in this book with a grill. You won't get that added flavor of smoke, but you'll have some fine eating.

halfway through the total cooking time, and start basting it at the same time that you turn it.

Smoker method: Cook the pork shoulder, at a temperature between 230 and 250°F, for 1½ hours per pound or until its internal temperature reaches 170 to 180°F. Turn the meat halfway through the total cooking time. Start basting it at the same time that you turn it.

For either method: Brush with your finishing sauce during the last 30 minutes of the cooking process.

In the oven: Roast the meat at 350°F, covered, for 3 to 4 hours, basting occasionally, and glaze with a finishing sauce during the last half hour of cooking.

Brisket

Brisket is cut from the breast of the steer. At best, it is a tough, fatty cut of beef, but that's what makes it perfect for barbecue. A whole brisket will weigh 7 to 12 pounds. You can marinate it in the refrigerator for up to 24 hours, but 5 to 7 hours should be enough. When barbecued, the meat will have shrunk considerably and will have a dark crust that resembles a meteorite on the outside, with moist, tender meat on the inside.

Covered grill method: Place the charcoal on one half of the lower grate, and place a disposable aluminum pan (available at most grocery stores) on the other half. Start with 2 to 2½ pounds of charcoal. Put soaked wood chips in the foil pan, and place the brisket on the upper grate, away from the fire and over the pan. Cover the grill, and cook the brisket at a temperature between 230 and 250°F, for 2 hours per pound, adding more wood chips after half an hour. Turn the brisket about halfway through the total cooking time, and start basting it at the same time that you turn it.

Remove the brisket, and let it rest for at least 15 minutes. Then slice and serve it.

Smoker method: Cook the brisket for 2 hours per pound, turning it halfway through the total cooking time. Start basting the ribs at the same time that you turn them. Smoke the ribs at a temperature between 230 and 250°F.

Remove the brisket, and let it rest for at least 15 minutes. Then slice and serve it.

For either method: Brush with with your finishing sauce during the last 30 minutes of the cooking process.

In the oven: Roast the meat at 250°F for 1 to 1¼ hours per pound.

Now go and have some fun.

1

Basic Ingredients

An Exploration of Spices,
Seasonings, Mustards,
Oils, and Vinegars

In the world of barbecue, as in any kind of cooking, the more you learn about your ingredients, the better cook you become! You can't choose a recipe to follow, much less develop your own recipes, if you don't know what to expect from the ingredients you'll be using. So get to know your ingredients, their background, their flavors, their aromas.

■ Spices and Seasonings ■

Spices are the basis for flavor in barbecue. They are gathered all over the world and have changed the history of the world. In ancient times they were a source of—and their use was a sign of—great wealth. The quest for spices has caused wars and spawned new nations. If you ever get a chance to read the history of spices, do so—it's fascinating. You will meet people like Attila the Hun, Marco Polo, Christopher Columbus, Napoleon, and many more voyagers of the world.

Once you have a good understanding of spices, you can make your own seasoning mixes—to season your foods with before you cook, to use as a barbecue rub, or even to serve at the table in place of, or in addition to, salt and pepper.

Master Class: Spices and Seasonings

Before you can create your own championship sauces and rubs, you need to be familiar with the spices that provide the flavor for your sauces. There are several steps to learning about spices and developing your taste buds and your olfactory senses. First, you have to read about spices and taste them so that you can identify them. Then you should find a recipe that uses the spice you want to learn about, and notice what it tastes like when you are cooking with it.

STEP ONE: KNOW YOUR SPICES.

What is a spice? I'm going to give you some straight definitions right out of the old dictionary.

spice *n.* **1.a.** Any of various pungent, aromatic plant substances, such as cinnamon or nutmeg, used to flavor foods or beverages. **b.** These substances considered as a group. **2.** Something that adds zest or flavor.

pungent *adj.* **1.a.** Affecting the organs of taste and smell with a sharp, acrid sensation. **b.** Not sweet. **2.a.** Penetrating, biting, or caustic. **b.** To the point; sharp. **3.** Affecting the organs of taste or smell with a strong and often harsh sensation; sharp, piquant, biting, or stinging.

piquant *adj.* Pleasantly pungent or tart in taste; spicy.

aromatic *adj.* Having a pleasant odor.

Some people will not understand putting herbs and spices in the same categories. For that matter, they may think I'm nuts for including garlic, onions, oranges, and lemons in this spice section. But for our barbecue-cooking purposes, if something is a plant substance that flavors our food, it's a spice.

STEP TWO: GET TO KNOW THE BARBECUE SPICES.

Now that we know what spices *are,* let's decide *which* spices make good barbecue. That exact question was posed to the readers of the Kansas City Barbecue Society's monthly *KC Bull Sheet,* along with the readers of *The National Barbecue News,* two of the favorite publications among barbecue aficionados. The responses revealed that barbecuers use a whole host of different spices and have very different ideas about which ones are good for barbecue. And that's as it should be: you are the one who has to be pleased with your own barbecue.

Read about all the spices that flavor barbecue. There are about thirty of them. If possible, do this in the kitchen so you can taste and sniff as you go.

Allspice: The allspice berry resembles an oversized, reddish brown peppercorn. Its flavor and aroma suggest a pungent and spicy blend of cloves, cinnamon, and nutmeg. Allspice adds zest to both savory and sweet dishes, including sauces (particularly tomato-based ones), marinades, relishes, and preserves, baked goods, and stews. It combines well with other spices. It is also called Jamaican pepper. Allspice comes whole or ground.

Basil/sweet basil: A native of India, basil is an annual culinary herb in temperate climates. It comes fresh and dried, leaf or ground. The soft green leaves are aromatic, with a pungent, licorice-like flavor. It is used in tomato sauces and also with poultry and fish.

Bay leaf: The evergreen bay shrub or laurel is native to southern Europe. It comes as a dark green leaf, crushed or ground, and it's very potent and aromatic. Bay leaves are not used very much in today's cooking, which is a shame because they add some great flavors to sauces, stews, and soups.

Cayenne: Red pepper, finely ground. Cayenne pepper is a variety of dried red capsicum peppers (chiles). It varies in color from orange-red to red, depending on the chiles used to prepare it. It also varies in its heat intensity, but it is always hot!

Celery seed: Celery seed is the fruit of wild celery, which is also known as lovage. The tiny seed is very pungent, with a pronounced celery smell. It tastes warm, with a hint of nutmeg and parsley, and is available ground or as a salt.

Chile powder: One or more dried and ground chile peppers, such as ancho, mulato, or pasilla, with no other spices.

Chiles, crushed: Crushed chiles can be a combination of several hot varieties that are dried and crushed whole, including the seeds but not (in the good-quality ones) the stems. Crushed red peppers are a good flavor addition to barbecue sauces, and they create more heat.

Chili powder: A blend of several dried peppers with cumin, garlic, oregano, cayenne, and paprika. Chili powder is also called chili seasoning.

Cilantro: Also known as Chinese or Mexican parsley, cilantro has small, fragile green leaves and thin stems. It has a slightly musty or soapy aroma, much different from parsley and more aromatic. It can be purchased in dry-leaf form or fresh, but the dry form has lost a lot of flavor.

Cinnamon: The dried, aromatic bark of the tropical Asian evergreen tree *(Cinnamomum cassia)*. It's a dark reddish brown and has a robust, warm, sweet flavor. It comes in sticks, in chunks, or ground.

Cloves: The dried buds of a tropical evergreen tree, native to the Moluccas (formerly the Spice Islands) and other warm regions. The dark nail-shaped clove is picked before it is ripe and then sun-dried. Because it is picked by hand, it is one of the world's most expensive spices. Cloves are sold whole or ground. They are very aromatic with a warm, sweet, almost peppery flavor.

> ### Spices—Whole or Ground?
>
> Whole spices that you grind yourself will have more flavor than spices you buy already ground. Use a clean coffee mill or a spice mill to grind spices and only spices. To clean a mill, grind up some white rice. The rice will attract the little pieces of spices.

Coriander: The seed of the cilantro plant. It is sold whole or ground. It has a mild, sweet flavor, with a lemony to orange taste. Coriander is good in any tomato sauce.

Cumin seed: An aromatic seed of a plant in the parsley family, the aroma of cumin is quite pronounced, with a very pungent flavor, spicy and sharp. It's an essential flavor in Mexican, Indian, and Middle Eastern cooking.

Dill weed: Also a member of the parsley family, dill comes both fresh and dried. The soft, feathery leaves have a refreshing, cool, buttery quality. Dill weed is usually used with fish or chicken.

Fennel seed: This seed is warm and fragrant, with a strong anise- or licorice-like flavor. The small, yellowish brown seeds are good on fresh fish, in sausage, and on pork. The seeds can be purchased whole, cracked, or ground.

Garlic: A member of the lily family, garlic is a single bulb with numerous cloves wrapped in a thin, papery outer skin. Garlic can be purchased fresh or in granulated, salt, or powdered forms. The pungent aroma and flavor of garlic make it one of our most valuable seasonings for savory dishes. Garlic is a good seasoning for any kind of meat, seafood, poultry, vegetable—any food, except maybe desserts. It's one of my favorite spices.

Ginger: One of the oldest and most popular spices, ginger has been cultivated for more than three thousand years. It is a knobby root used extensively in most Asian cuisines, where it is considered almost as important as salt. In my opinion, its place in barbecue is also essential. Ginger has a pungent, hot-sweet flavor with a very pleasant aroma. It is sold fresh, ground, pickled, or candied. Ginger is good in sauces and seasonings for meat or poultry.

Lemon: Lemons are generally too sour to eat out of hand, but their lively tartness sharpens other flavors and gives a lift to all kinds of foods. Lemon can be purchased fresh or as a frozen concentrate; you can also buy lemon juice, lemon zest (peels), and lemon powder. If you have trouble finding lemon powder, use a commercial lemonade mix (or see page 30).

Monosodium glutamate: Commonly known as MSG, this flavor enhancer is widely used in commercially prepared meat or fish and in home kitchens under the brand name Accent or a variety of other names. MSG's white, crystalline powder is the salt of glutamic acid and occurs naturally in sugar beets, soybeans, and seaweed. It can also be manufactured from sugar cane starch or molasses. MSG has no flavor of its own but is reputed to intensify the flavor of foods cooked with it. How MSG works is not clear. Western scientists think it stimulates taste receptors (taste buds), and Asian scientists believe it stimulates a fifth taste beyond salty, sweet, sour, or bitter.

A general caution regarding MSG: Although MSG is on the Food and Drug Administration's generally recognized as safe (GRAS) list, controversy regarding its safety has arisen. Some people are sensitive to MSG, and experience symptoms such

Fresh Spices Pack More Punch

You won't get the best results with rubs and seasoning mixes made from stale spices, so always buy spices in small quantities—only what you can use within six months. Store spices in airtight jars in a cool, dry place.

as chest pain, facial pressure, swelling of the tongue, a burning sensation, or even difficulty in breathing when they eat something with MSG in it. Sensitivity to MSG is also known as Chinese Food Syndrome, because of the use of MSG in Asian cooking. Studies show that the percentage of the population that is sensitive to MSG is very small.

Mustard seed and powder: Known for thousands of years, mustard has always had many uses. It comes in a variety of colors: yellow (white), brown, and black. Unlike many spices, ground mustard seed has virtually no aroma or character, but when you moisten it, it comes alive. Mustard in one form or another is good with any kind of meat, poultry, or fish. It's a good accompaniment to sauces and rubs, and it blends well with other seasonings. The more you can learn about the mysteries of mustard and the way it interacts with foods, the better a cook you'll become.

Mustard comes ground, powdered, or whole. You will see ground mustard seed listed in this book as "dry mustard powder." Some people also call it "mustard flour." The yellow and brown seeds are easy to find; the black seeds can usually be found in Indian grocery stores.

Nutmeg and mace: *Myristica fragrans* produces two distinct spices—nutmeg and mace. They are the seed of an apricot-type fruit. The fragile webbed outer membrane is mace, and the kernel of the seed is the nutmeg. Both spices are dried before we get them. Nutmeg and mace are very overpowering—a little goes a long way. Mace and nutmeg are similar in aroma and taste, but mace is more refined. The aroma is rich, fresh, and warm. The taste is sweetish in nutmeg and more bitter in mace.

Onion: Considered one of the universal spices, onion is a seasoning in almost all cuisines and is also a very popular vegetable. Onions can be purchased fresh, dried, minced, powdered, or granulated and as onion salt.

Orange: The orange comes in a variety of flavors from sweet to bitter and from orange to red in color. The orange is valued for its juice and its aromatic peel, or zest.

Oregano: A member of the mint family. There are two main varieties of oregano sold in the United States: the European and the Mexican. Mexican oregano is the more pungent of the two. European oregano is milder and can usually be found fresh at the grocery store. You can also buy it ground or in a dried-leaf variety. Cooking oregano can make it bitter, so if you're going to use it in a sauce or stew, make a tea and use it that way or add it during the last few minutes of cooking.

Paprika: Paprika is a capsicum pepper that is dried and ground. It varies from orange to dark red, and it varies in pungency from very mild (sweet) to half-sweet to hot. Hungarian paprika is considered the best and is dark red. The Spanish version, which has virtually no taste, is more orange in color. Paprika is used primarily for color in barbecue and in most cooking.

Parsley: Parsley is a cultivated herb, used as a seasoning or a garnish. It is sold as fresh or dried leaves.

Pepper: *Piper nigrum,* "the spice of the world," is the most widely used spice in the Western world and the most misunderstood spice there is. Growing up I can remember hearing, "Don't put so much pepper on that piece of meat or it will be too hot to eat." First of all, pepper is one of the best flavor enhancers there is. It's not hot, if you have any tolerance for heat at all. It is also very flavorful. Pepper has a warm, woody smell that is fresh, pungent, and agreeably aromatic. White pepper tastes hotter and less subtle than black. Green pepper has a clean fresh taste and is not as pungent or hot.

Pepper is sold in various stages of maturity, from fresh green to black, from whole to ground. Green peppercorns are immature peppercorns, which are usually dried or canned in vinegar or a brine. Black peppercorns are mature berries. White peppercorns are the dried berries from black peppercorns that have had the black hulls removed after being soaked in a brine to soften them. Pink peppercorns, from the *Baies* rose plant, have a brittle outer shell enclosing a small seed. They are often sold along with the black and white peppercorns, but they belong to a different family and do not have the same pungent taste as the other two. The best black varieties are Tellicherry and Malabar, and a good white variety is Muntok.

Poultry seasoning: Usually a blend of sage, thyme, marjoram, oregano, savory, onion, black pepper, and celery seed or other herbs, poultry seasoning is always in ground or powdered form.

Rosemary: A perennial evergreen shrub, rosemary has green and gray needlelike leaves. Rosemary complements beef, lamb, pork, poultry, fish, soups, salads, vegetables—you name it. As a seasoning, its flavor combines both strong and subtle qualities. Rosemary is pungent, somewhat piny, and mintlike, and it has a slightly gingery finish.

Sage: A member of the mint family, sage is a pungent herb that comes in many varieties. It has an aggressive aroma and flavor, slightly musty or camphorlike, lemony, and pleasantly bitter. Sage can be purchased fresh or dried, in whole or crumbled leaves, or rubbed or ground.

Thyme: Thyme is another member of the mint family and one of the most widely used herbs in the cook's pantry. Its subtle flavor and aroma make it a background herb, rarely the major seasoning in a dish, but one that gives complexity to countless culinary preparations. Thyme can be purchased fresh, as dried leaves, or ground.

We have only scratched the surface of spices, but the ones that we've previewed will help you create world championship barbecue! And if there are other spices that you think should be included on the list, by all means, add them.

STEP THREE: CREATE A MASTER BARBECUE FLAVORPRINT SPICE RECIPE.

Think of curry powder. It's got all those wonderful hot and sweet spices from India. You taste a dish that has a little curry powder in it, and you know you are tasting the flavorprint, or unique cooking, of India. You can work the same magic for barbecue. You just put the flavors together that say "barbecue."

Barbecue Spice can be as varied as the people who cook barbecue. But as a starting point, you want some heat, some pungent flavors, some sweet flavors, some aromatics. Here is a basic recipe to get you started. Add to it, subtract from it, make it your own.

Master Barbecue Spice

Makes about 1/3 cup

2   tablespoons paprika
1   tablespoon dried light brown sugar*
2   teaspoons dry mustard powder
½   teaspoon garlic powder
½   teaspoon ground celery seed
½   teaspoon sea salt**
½   teaspoon ground thyme
½   teaspoon ground coriander
½   teaspoon ground marjoram
¼   teaspoon cayenne

Combine all of the ingredients, and blend well. Store in an airtight jar in a cool, dry place for 2 to 3 months, or in the freezer for up to 6 months.

■ **How to Use It:** Use Master Barbecue Spice as an all-purpose rub for meat, poultry, or fish, or to add spice to a mop or sauce.

*Note: To dry brown sugar, place it on a cookie sheet and air-dry it for 2 to 3 hours, mixing it every 30 to 45 minutes, until it's dry. Sift before using.

**Note: I recommend using non-iodized salt, as iodized salt can leave spots or streaks on the meat.

The Baron's High Octane Seasoning

With all of these hot and pungent ingredients, such as onion, garlic, curry, horseradish, and white pepper, this seasoning really packs a punch.

Makes about 1/4 cup

1   tablespoon sea salt
2   teaspoons onion powder
1   teaspoon ground celery seed
1   teaspoon dried dill weed
1   teaspoon orange powder
1   teaspoon garlic powder
½   teaspoon curry powder
½   teaspoon horseradish powder
½   teaspoon white pepper
½   teaspoon dry mustard powder
½   teaspoon powdered sweet red pepper
½   teaspoon dried basil leaves
½   teaspoon dried marjoram leaves
½   teaspoon dried rosemary, minced
¼   teaspoon ground oregano
¼   teaspoon ground thyme

Combine all of the ingredients, and blend well. Store in an airtight jar in a cool, dry place for 2 to 3 months, or in the freezer for up to 6 months.

■ **How to Use It:** You can use this blend like salt and pepper—and that means on just about any savory food you want to punch up with extra flavor.

Flavorprints

A *flavorprint* is a list of spices that distinguishes a national cuisine, such as French, Mexican, or Italian.

Why a *barbecue* flavorprint? Barbecue aficionado Mason Steinberg, of Mason's Old Mill Barbecue in Omaha, Nebraska, states it best: "We've gone through all these ethnic foods, and now all of a sudden, we're discovering our roots. These roots happen to be BARBECUE!"

A Barbecue Flavorprint

allspice	curry powder	paprika
barbecue spice	dill weed	parsley
bay leaf	dry mustard	pepper
Cajun spice blend	fennel seed	poultry seasoning
cayenne pepper	garlic	rosemary
celery seed	ginger	sage
chili powder	lemon	salt
cilantro	MSG (monosodium	seasoned salt
cinnamon	glutamate)	sugar
cloves	nutmeg	sweet basil
coriander	onion	tenderizers
crushed chiles	orange	thyme
cumin seed	oregano	

This is my flavorprint of barbecue! I based my list on spices that I associate with barbecue. You will notice I've included only the basic spices. For instance, when using garlic, the form could be salt, granulated, powder, or fresh. There are many spices that you can use that are not in my flavorprint, and that's all right. The flavorprint is just my own basic list of spices. Something else to keep in mind about barbecue flavorprints: all of them should include black pepper and onions.

Cajun Spice Blend

In this chapter's Master Class, there is a recipe for a Master Barbecue Spice Blend. That doesn't mean you have to use it every time you barbecue. Maybe you want to explore some different flavorprints. Cajun and creole cooking from Louisiana have spread throughout the States and abroad in recent years. Chiles, aromatic herbs, garlic, onion, mustard, and cumin are the major flavorings.

Makes about 1/3 cup

- 1 tablespoon paprika
- 2 teaspoons cayenne
- 2 teaspoons dry mustard powder
- 2 teaspoons salt
- 1 teaspoon black pepper
- 1 teaspoon garlic powder
- 1 teaspoon ground sage
- ½ teaspoon white pepper
- ½ teaspoon onion powder
- ½ teaspoon ground cumin
- ½ teaspoon ground thyme
- ½ teaspoon ground oregano

Combine all of the ingredients, and blend well. Store in an airtight jar in a cool, dry place for 2 to 3 months, or in the freezer for up to 6 months.

■ **How to Use It:** You can use this spice blend as a rub or you can add it to any dish that you want to have a Cajun flavor—soups, stews, roasts, you name it.

Jerk Seasoning

Jamaica is famous for its jerk barbecue—a combination of sweet and searing hot flavors. Jerk barbecue is a thriving roadside fast-food industry on the island. Pork and chicken are the meats most commonly found jerked in Jamaica, but sometimes fish is seasoned this way, too. The ground habanero pepper—or Scotch bonnets, as they are called in Jamaica—may take some tracking down (see Resources), but it's a signature chile—very, very hot, but also floral in flavor.

Makes about 1/2 cup

- 1 tablespoon granulated onion
- 1 tablespoon onion powder
- 1 tablespoon ground allspice
- 1 tablespoon sugar
- 1 tablespoon black pepper
- 1 tablespoon cayenne
- 1 tablespoon garlic salt
- ½ teaspoon ground thyme
- ½ teaspoon ground cinnamon
- ¼ teaspoon ground habanero chile
- ¼ teaspoon ground nutmeg
- ¼ teaspoon powdered bay leaf

Combine all the ingredients, and blend well. Store in an airtight jar in a cool, dry place for 2 to 3 months, or in the freezer for up to 6 months.

■ **How to Use It:** Use the seasoning as a rub for pork, chicken, or fish.

West Indian Curry Powder

There are hundreds of different curry powders from various regions in India. Curries range from pastes and powders to a mixture of whole spices. Some are hot or medium-hot, others are mild and fragrant. This particular blend is characteristic of the cooking of western India.

Makes about 1/4 cup

- 1 tablespoon ground turmeric
- 2 teaspoons ground ginger
- 2 teaspoons ground coriander
- 1 teaspoon ground cinnamon
- 1 teaspoon ground anise seed
- 1 teaspoon finely ground black pepper
- 1 teaspoon dry mustard powder
- 1 teaspoon ground fenugreek

Combine all of the ingredients, and blend well. Store in an airtight jar in a cool, dry place for 2 to 3 months, or in the freezer for up to 6 months.

■ **How to Use It:** Use it any way you would use a commercial curry powder.

Seasoned Salt

Seasoned salt is salt blended with any number of spices and herbs. I use seasoned salt a lot in my cooking. It adds that much more flavor than plain salt. This is handy to keep in a shaker on the table.

Makes about 3/4 cup

- ½ cup salt
- ¼ cup paprika
- 2 teaspoons dry mustard powder
- 1 teaspoon garlic powder
- 1 teaspoon curry powder
- 1 teaspoon onion powder
- ½ teaspoon ground thyme
- ¼ teaspoon ground oregano

A Fair Shake for Salt

Some wit once said that "salt is what makes things taste bad when it isn't in them." That's a pretty good starting point for understanding what salt does: It makes food taste good; it brings out the flavor of the food.

All of the salt we use in cooking comes from the sea— either from salt mines that contain salt deposits laid down by dried-up seas from ancient times or from a process of evaporating seawater. Then it is refined.

Table salt has small crystals. Usually it has additives to keep it from clumping when exposed to moisture.

Iodized salt is table salt that has iodine added to prevent a disease called hypothyroidism. You use it just like table salt.

Kosher salt has larger crystals. Most cooks say it provides better flavor and texture.

Sea salt is evaporated from seawater. It is usually more expensive than other salts. You can get it fine-grained or coarse-grained. I think sea salt has better flavor than table salt, and I use it in many of my sauces.

Forget about using rock salt in recipes. It's best used in ice-cream makers and to bed down baked oysters and clams.

Seasoned salt is salt plus a flavoring like garlic, onion, or celery. I use a lot of seasoned salt in my barbecue for the extra flavor it offers.

Combine all of the ingredients, and blend well. Store in an airtight jar. This seasoned salt will keep for 2 to 3 months in a cool, dry place, or in the refrigerator for up to 6 months.

■ **How to Use It:** Use the seasoned salt as you would use regular salt, in any savory dish you cook.

Chili Powder/Seasoning

Chili powder or seasoning is a blend of ground chiles and other spices.

Makes 3/4 cup

- ¼ cup ground ancho chile
- 2 tablespoons ground cumin
- 2 tablespoons paprika
- 1 tablespoon garlic powder
- 1 tablespoon salt
- 1 tablespoon ground coriander
- 2 teaspoons cayenne
- 1 teaspoon ground oregano

Combine all of the ingredients, and blend well. Store in an airtight jar in a cool, dry place for 2 to 3 months, or in the freezer for up to 6 months.

■ **How to Use It:** Use this seasoning any way you would use commercial chili powder.

Powdered Chiles Pack Heat and Flavor

You might think all ground dried red chiles just give off heat, but each one gives a subtly different flavor to a spice blend, sauce, or rub. Here's a list of some of the chiles you might want to sample. You can buy these chiles powdered, but you can also make your own powder from any dried chile. I advise using a spice mill which you keep for chiles only. I've included their heat ratings in Scoville units.

Ancho chiles (2,000 Scoville units): A mild and very fragrant chile. It has a traditional Mexican flavor—it is the chile you expect to taste in tamales and chilis. Some people describe anchos as sweet and fruity.

Cayenne red pepper (40,000 Scoville units): You can find cayenne pretty easily in the supermarket. It's a good choice for adding heat and a fairly subtle chile flavor.

Chipotle peppers (15,000 Scoville units): Smoke-dried jalapeño peppers, chipotles add smoke and a mild heat to cooked foods. They are red ripe jalapeños which are slowly dried in smoke so the flavor is rich, smoky, and hot, but not searing hot.

Crushed red peppers (20,000 Scoville units): The crushed red chile pepper flakes you find on the table at the local pizzeria are probably crushed California red peppers. They are moderately hot and moderately flavorful—provided you get them freshly dried.

Jalapeño peppers (35,000 Scoville units): You can get these peppers fresh, crushed, or powdered. Jalapeños can be as hot as cayenne peppers, but their heat leaves the mouth sooner. Also, you can cook the heat out of a jalapeño.

No-Salt Lemon Herbal Seasoning

You don't have to give up good eating just because the doctor says to cut back on the salt. No-salt seasonings are blends of herbs and spices to take the place of salt. You can use this blend in just about everything you cook, even barbecue rubs. As a rub, this seasoning mix doesn't contain much heat—just a little white pepper and cayenne—but it derives a lot of flavor from the lemon powder and garlic.

Makes about 6 tablespoons

1 tablespoon lemon powder
1 tablespoon granulated garlic
1 tablespoon dried parsley flakes
2 teaspoons dried dill weed
2 teaspoons dried basil leaves
2 teaspoons white pepper
1 teaspoon dry mustard powder
1 teaspoon granulated onion
½ teaspoon ground celery seed
½ teaspoon dried marjoram
½ teaspoon crushed rosemary
½ teaspoon cayenne

Combine all of the ingredients, and blend well. Store in an airtight jar in a cool, dry place for 2 to 3 months, or in the freezer for up to 6 months.

■ How to Use It: Use this as a seasoning or as a rub.

Lemon Powder

Lemon powder is the dried outer peel of the lemon, ground to a fine powder. It should have bright yellow color and strong lemon flavor. Buy it in small quantities—enough for three months, and after that, replenish your supplies. If you can't find the powder locally, you can order it from Penzeys, Ltd., P.O. Box 933, Muskego, WI 53150; (414) 679-7207.

No-Salt Zesty Herbal Seasoning

You may notice that this blend seems similar to the previous one. It is, but the addition of ground chiles, black pepper, and more cayenne gives this seasoning mix more heat, and adding the cumin and the sage gives it more punch. I like to use both of these no-salt blends as a barbecue rub as well as in everyday cooking.

Makes 1/2 cup

1 tablespoon granulated garlic
1 tablespoon granulated onion
2 teaspoons ground dried New Mexico chiles
2 teaspoons fresh-ground black pepper
2 teaspoons dried dill weed
2 teaspoons lemon powder
2 teaspoons rubbed sage
1 teaspoon ground cumin
1 teaspoon ground celery seed
1 teaspoon dried basil
1 teaspoon dried marjoram
1 teaspoon dry mustard powder
1 teaspoon dried parsley flakes
1 teaspoon crushed dried rosemary
1 teaspoon cayenne

Combine all of the ingredients, and blend well. Store in an airtight jar in a cool, dry place for 2 to 3 months, or in the freezer for up to 6 months.

■ **How to Use It:** Use this as a seasoning or as a rub.

■ Mustards ■

Mustard is one of my passions in life. I don't make mustards as much as I used to because they are so addictive. Homemade mustards are good on all meats—barbecued, roasted, or fried—on potato chips, pretzels, vegetables, sausages, hot dogs, and even fingers. I can make a batch of mustard and sit down and eat it.

The first recipe in this section is a mustard sauce that I paint on my barbecue before I season it with my barbecue seasoning or rub. Of all the barbecuing recommendations that I make, this is one of the procedures that I consider to be the most important, but it is the one that students tend to skip! What does the mustard do, and how does it taste on your finished product? The mustard, or mustard sauce, seals and moistens the meat. The vinegars in it interact with the enzymes of the meat. They also help your rub stick to the meat. As far as how the mustard tastes, it enhances the flavor of the meat without giving it the flavor of mustard. All it does is work with your barbecue to make it better.

You can use all of the mustards in this section in a similar way—paint them on your meats before adding the rubs. You can also serve the Coarse Ground Mustard, Sweet German-Style Mustard, Dijon-Style Mustard, and Green Peppercorn Mustard as condiments.

Sam's Special Mustard Sauce

This first recipe I got from Sam Higgins, one of the finest barbecuers that Texas has ever produced. I first met Crazy Sam, as he was known in those days, when Rich Davis, the creator of K.C. Masterpiece Barbecue Sauce, called me and wanted to know if I'd be interested in tasting brisket that had been mesquite-smoked for twenty-six hours. Well, to put it mildly, I am not a fan of mesquite-smoked anything. For grilling steaks it's great, but for smoking, I don't think so. Rich explained that Sam was bringing two briskets and asked if I would like to come over to his house for dinner and try some.

Well, my love of brisket far outweighs my dislike for mesquite, so I was game. To this day—and that was in 1986—I believe that was some of the finest brisket that I have ever put into my mouth, and it started with a mustard sauce similar to this first recipe. Sam does have a barbecue cookbook out, but I don't know if it's still in print. Anyway, its title is *I'm Glad I Ate When I Did 'Cause I'm Not Hungry Now.* If you can find a copy, you'll see that it's a fun and informative book.

Makes about 5 cups

1	12-ounce can flat beer
4	cups prepared yellow mustard
1	tablespoon Louisiana-style hot sauce
½	cup dark brown sugar, packed
1	teaspoon sea salt
1	teaspoon black pepper

Combine all of the ingredients in a nonreactive bowl. Use a wire whisk to blend all of the ingredients.

Store the mustard in an airtight jar in the refrigerator. It will keep for several months.

■ **How to Use It:** Prepare brisket, ribs, pork, or chicken, then paint it with the mustard sauce and season it with your rub. Barbecue as you normally would, using the indirect method. Remember this is not a dipping sauce, but a cooking sauce.

■ **Variations:** You could replace the beer with some lemon juice, use some booze for the beer, or use Dijon mustard for the American mustard.

Uncle Len LeCluyse's Mustard

Uncle Len, my mother's brother, was a fabulous football player when he went to Notre Dame. He loved good food, and when I was young he taught me how to make blood and liver sausage, which several of my uncles, my grandfather, and I used to make together. Uncle Len knew that I liked mustard, but couldn't find anyone who would share their recipe. So he gave me this one, and I've been making it ever since.

Makes about 1 1/2 cups

2   1¼-ounce cans Colman's dry mustard powder
1   cup white vinegar
3   eggs
1   cup white sugar

Combine the mustard and vinegar in a nonreactive bowl. Beat with a wire whisk until the mustard is completely dissolved. Let the mixture sit overnight.

Beat the eggs lightly, add the sugar, and mix well. Combine the egg mixture with the vinegar mixture in a nonreactive saucepan, and bring to a boil. Reduce the heat and simmer, stirring constantly, until the desired thickness is reached.

Store the mustard in an airtight jar in the refrigerator..

■ **How to Use It:** Use the mustard warm or chilled, as a condiment or as a sauce to paint on beef or chicken before sprinkling on a rub.

> Brushing olive oil or prepared mustard on the meat that you are going to barbecue helps your rub or seasoning stick.

Geography of Mustard

American mustard: The standard bright-yellow American-ballpark mustard (also called salad mustard) is made from yellow mustard seeds, sugar, vinegar, and turmeric (for color). American mustard is smooth and mild.

Chinese mustard: Made from dry mustard and water or vinegar, this mustard paste is hot and bright yellow in color. Its flavor fades fast.

Dijon mustard: Spicier and more pungent than American mustard, Dijon mustards (made in Dijon, France) and Dijon-style mustards (made anywhere, but in the style of Dijon mustards) are smooth in texture and a pale grayish yellow in color. They are made from brown mustard seeds, white wine, unfermented grape juice, and seasonings.

English mustard: Found in pubs and served with cheese and crackers, English mustard is bright yellow and very hot. It is made from both yellow and brown mustard seeds, flour, and turmeric.

German mustard: This mustard can range in color from bright yellow to brown. It can range in texture from smooth to coarse and in flavor from hot to mild. It is usually a little sweet.

Coarse Ground Mustard

You can use any mustard seed for this one—yellow, brown, or black, or a combination. I usually use brown mustard seeds for the extra bite.

Makes about 1 cup

¼ cup whole mustard seeds
¼ cup red wine
¼ cup red wine vinegar
¼ cup water
2 tablespoons clover honey
1 garlic clove, pressed
1½ teaspoons sea salt
¼ teaspoon ground allspice
¼ teaspoon finely ground black pepper
⅛ teaspoon powdered bay leaf

Combine the mustard seeds, red wine, and red wine vinegar in a nonreactive bowl. Set aside to soak for 3 to 4 hours.

Put the mixture in a food processor fitted with a steel blade, or in a blender. Process to blend. Add the water, honey, garlic, salt, allspice, pepper, and bay leaf. Blend to mix well, but retain the fairly coarse texture.

Scrape into the top of a double boiler, and cook over simmering water for 5 to 10 minutes, or until the mixture reaches a desired thickness. Let cool slightly.

Store the mustard in an airtight jar in the refrigerator. It will keep for several months.

■ **How to Use It:** Use this mustard chilled or at room temperature. Try it as a condiment or as a sauce to paint on beef or pork before sprinkling on a rub.

Sweet German-Style Mustard

When I make this mustard, I usually use a combination of yellow and brown mustard seeds, but you can use any type of seed or combination of seeds you like.

Makes about 2 cups

- ¼ cup whole mustard seeds
- 5 tablespoons dry mustard powder
- ½ cup hot water
- 1 cup cider vinegar
- ¼ cup cold water
- 2 large slices of onion
- 2 tablespoons brown sugar, packed
- 2 tablespoons clover honey
- 1½ teaspoons sea salt
- 2 garlic cloves, pressed
- ¼ teaspoon ground allspice
- ¼ teaspoon ground cinnamon
- ¼ teaspoon dried dill weed
- ¼ teaspoon ground cloves
- 3 tablespoons light corn syrup

Combine the mustard seeds, mustard powder, hot water, and ½ cup of the vinegar in a nonreactive bowl. Set the mixture aside to soak for 3 to 4 hours.

Combine the remaining ½ cup vinegar with the cold water, onion, brown sugar, honey, salt, garlic, allspice, cinnamon, dill weed, and cloves in a saucepan. Bring to a boil. Boil for 1 minute, cover, and let sit for 1 hour.

Scrape the soaked mustard mixture into a food processor fitted with a steel blade, or into a blender. Strain the spice infusion (the water, onion, and spice mixture) into the mustard, pressing on the onion to get all of the spices and juice out of it. Process the mustard until the consistency is a coarse purée with a discernible graininess.

Pour the mustard purée into the top of a double boiler over simmering water. Cook, stirring often, for 10 minutes, until the mixture reaches a desired thickness. Remove from the heat, and then add the corn syrup. Blend well. Let cool slightly.

Store the mustard in an airtight jar in the refrigerator. It will keep for several months.

■ **How to Use It:** This is an especially tasty table mustard to serve on sandwiches. Serve it chilled or at room temperature. It can also be painted onto beef or pork before you sprinkle on a barbecue rub.

Dijon-Style Mustard

The French government wouldn't let me call this a Dijon mustard because it isn't made with brown or black mustard seeds, and I'm not from Dijon. The heck with it. This is a great mustard no matter what you call it.

Makes about 3/4 cup

¼ cup yellow mustard seeds
1 tablespoon dry mustard powder
⅓ cup cold water
⅓ cup white wine vinegar
1 tablespoon light corn syrup
2 teaspoons sugar
1 teaspoon sea salt
½ teaspoon white pepper
⅛ teaspoon ground allspice

Grind the mustard seeds to a fine meal in a spice mill or a clean coffee grinder. Place in a small bowl, add the dry mustard and water, and blend together. Let sit, uncovered, for 3 hours at room temperature.

In a food processor fitted with a steel blade, combine the mustard seed mixture with the vinegar, syrup, sugar, salt, pepper, and allspice. Process to a smooth texture, scraping down the sides of the container several times. Let sit overnight at room temperature before using. Adjust the seasoning if necessary.

Store the mustard in an airtight jar in the refrigerator. It will keep indefinitely.

■ **How to Use It:** Use chilled or at room temperature, as a condiment or in any way you would use a commercial Dijon mustard (in salad dressings or sauces, for example). Or paint it onto beef or pork before sprinkling on a rub.

Green Peppercorn Mustard

Green peppercorns. How do you define their light, somewhat pungent, taste? This mustard is a good way to get familiar with them.

Makes 1 cup

1 cup Dijon-style mustard
2 green peppercorns, finely ground
¼ teaspoon dried tarragon, crumbled
⅛ teaspoon ground allspice
⅛ teaspoon ground cinnamon
⅛ teaspoon white pepper
   Salt to taste

Combine all of the ingredients, and blend well. Adjust the seasonings if desired. Store the mustard in an airtight jar in the refrigerator. It will keep indefinitely.

■ **How to Use It:** Use chilled or at room temperature. This is another good table mustard. Try brushing it onto chicken before grilling.

■ Oils and Flavored Oils ■

Oil is a lot of things to food: it's a lubricant, a moisturizer, a carrier of seasonings and spices. You can fry with it, and it plays an important role in browning foods.

The discovery of oil predates recorded history. Ancient peoples all over the world discovered that they could press vegetables and nuts to extract oil. In India, the ground nut (peanut) and mustard seed were crushed; in the South Seas, it was the coconut. In Africa, the fruit of the oil palm was crushed to yield oil. This oil could moisturize rough skin, burn in lamps, and grease a cooking pan.

Oil picks up flavors when it is heated, and this is one of the properties that makes it great for use in barbecues. In a marinade, it also helps to replace some of the moisture in meat that has been drawn out by vinegar. Marinades are usually one part oil to one part vinegar. There the oil works to balance out the vinegar, while also adding moisture and flavoring. You can use oil in mops, too.

So what do you need to know about oil? Well, not all oil is created equal. Oils can be neutral in flavor (like canola or safflower oil), or they can have the distinctive flavor of the fruit or nut from which they are pressed (like olive oil or any nut oil). How an oil is made also affects flavor. Cold-pressed oils, which are mechanically squeezed out of the fruit, are the most flavorful—also the most expensive and the most perishable. You can taste the peanut in cold-pressed peanut oil, but you can't really pick up the flavor from most of the cheap domestic brands. The less expensive oils are extracted by means of chemicals, heat, water, or a combination of the three.

Olive oils are graded to indicate quality, with extra-virgin being the fruitiest tasting and the most expensive. Then, in order of descending quality, come superfine, fine, and virgin olive oils. Pure olive oil is the least expensive and will have the least olive flavor. It is not always necessary to use the finer grades.

Sometimes you want an oil to give a lot of flavor. Sesame oil has a strong sesame flavor that makes it perfect for some oriental marinades. Olive oil also goes well in marinades that have Mediterranean flavors, such as garlic or basil.

When you want an oil to pack a lot of flavor, you can use a flavored oil, also called an infusion oil. Flavored oils can be used in marinades, salad dressings, and sauces. To make a flavored oil, you gently heat the oil, add herbs or another flavor, and let the oil steep for a while, as if you were making tea. Once the flavors have steeped, thoroughly strain the oil, and pour it into a clean jar.

Garlic Oil

I say go the distance with this one and use a high-quality extra-virgin olive oil for the oil. But in truth, you can use any oil that's edible.

Makes 1 cup

1   cup oil (extra-virgin olive or any cooking oil)
6   garlic cloves, peeled

Place the oil and the garlic cloves in a saucepan over medium heat. Cook until the garlic turns golden. Watch carefully; don't let the garlic brown or it will have a bitter taste. Turn off the heat, and let the mixture cool to room temperature. Strain out the garlic cloves and any garlic debris. Pour the strained oil into a clean jar. Use it the same day.

■ **How to Use It:** Use this oil in any marinade for extra garlic flavor. It's good in salad dressings, too.

Porcini Mushroom Oil

This is great stuff—a poor man's truffle oil.

Makes 2 cups

- 12 dried porcini mushrooms
- ½ cup boiling water
- 2 cups olive oil

To rehydrate the mushrooms, put them in a saucepan or heatproof container, and pour the boiling water over the mushrooms. Let them sit for 15 to 20 minutes. Take the mushrooms out of the water, and pat dry.

Combine the mushrooms and oil in a saucepan, and heat over low heat for about 20 minutes. Set aside in a cool, dark place for 2 hours. Strain the oil through a fine mesh to remove the mushrooms and mushroom fragments. Pour the strained oil into a clean jar. Use it the same day.

■ **How to Use It:** Combine this oil with some red wine, and you have a fine marinade for a steak. This oil works well in most beef marinades. You can also use it for cooking most vegetables.

Spicy Asian Oil

I call this "instant Asian flavor in a bottle." You've got your toasted sesame flavor, and your chiles and peppercorns for heat. The garlic, ginger, and lemongrass add a touch of Southeast Asian flavor.

Makes about 2 cups

1½ cups sunflower or safflower oil
¾ cup whole dried chile pods (serranos, Thai chiles, or other dried chiles)
¼ cup sesame oil
7 garlic cloves
2 tablespoons chopped fresh gingerroot
1 tablespoon black peppercorns
2 stalks lemongrass,* with any dry leaves removed, cut into 2-inch pieces

Using the side of a knife, smash the cloves of garlic part way, but not so that they break into pieces. Combine all of the ingredients, including the garlic, in a saucepan. Cook over medium heat until the garlic turns golden brown. Remove from the heat, cover, and let cool to room temperature. Strain the mixture through a fine mesh. Pour the strained oil into a clean jar. Use it the same day.

■ **How to Use It:** This is a great oil to make if your cooking style includes stir-fries and other nonbarbecue efforts. You can use this on grilled foods, too—try brushing it on shrimp before grilling. Or, use it for extra punch in the Korean Beef Marinade (page 121).

*Note: Lemongrass can be purchased at Asian, natural food, health food, and well-stocked grocery stores. Use only the bottom 4 inches of the stalk.

In Japan, a five-dish meal almost always includes barbecue.

Zesty Lemon Oil

This is a great oil to brush on fish or poultry for the grill.

Makes about 1 quart

- 6 whole lemons, unpeeled with no blemishes, cut into thick slices
- 2 tablespoons coriander seeds
- 1 tablespoon black peppercorns
- 3 bay leaves
- 4 cups extra-virgin olive oil

In a straight-sided glass dish with a lid, layer the lemons, spreading the coriander, peppercorns, and bay leaves between the layers. Cover, and set aside for a few hours in a cool, dark place. Then cover the lemon mixture with the olive oil, and set aside for 3 to 4 days. Remove the lemons, and strain the oil through a fine mesh. Pour the oil into clean bottles and cover. Store the oil in the refrigerator for up to 1 week.

■ **How to Use It:** Brush this oil onto fish, shellfish, or chicken. Then sprinkle on a barbecue rub or seasoning, and grill. The seasoning will cling to the flesh and form a nice crust. Or, use the oil in any fish or poultry marinade.

Spicy Hot Chile Oil

If you like hot foods, this is a very versatile recipe. It has a lingering bite to it. If you want oil a little less pungent, start omitting peppers, but understand that each type of pepper gives you a different flavor in addition to its heat. You can increase the heat by slitting the sides of the fresh chiles before placing them in the oil.

Makes about 1 quart

- 4 cups peanut oil
- 12 jalapeños
- 6 serrano chiles
- 2 New Mexico chiles (or Anaheims), seeded and cut into 2-inch strips
- 1 habanero chile
- 2 teaspoons black peppercorns
- 2 garlic cloves, smashed

Place all of the ingredients in a nonreactive saucepan, cover, and cook over medium heat for 30 minutes. Reduce the heat to low, and cook for another 30 minutes. Remove the mixture from the heat, allow it to cool to room temperature, and strain the mixture through a fine mesh. Pour the oil into a clean jar, and use it the same day.

■ **How to Use It:** Use this oil in any marinade when you want instant heat.

■ Vinegars ■

Vinegar… Mother Nature's liquid gold! If you ever get a chance to study this discovery of ten thousand years ago, you'll find that besides being a condiment and a preservative, vinegar is nature's answer to almost any ailment. But that's another study—we are just looking at the cooking properties of vinegar.

vinegar *n.* An impure dilute solution of acetic acid obtained by fermentation beyond the alcohol stage and used as a condiment and preservative.

The word *vinegar* comes from the French words *vin,* meaning "wine," and *aigre,* meaning "sour," so you get the idea how it came about. You can make your own vinegar if you can find a source of vinegar "mother." This is a bacterial culture to which wine (white or red) is added. Just a tiny bit of mother is needed. When the mother is stored, preferably in a covered crock, it grows and begins to look like you're growing a piece of liver.

In a marinade or mop, the acid works as a flavor carrier of the spices. It also softens the texture of the item marinated, and that helps shorten the cooking time. More often than not, the acid used is vinegar. Vinegar is also used in a lot of barbecue sauces to balance out the sugar.

Which vinegar you use in your marinades or sauces will greatly affect their flavor. I generally use distilled white vinegar because I am looking for a sharp neutral flavor. But that's just my preference. Here's a list of vinegars you might want to try.

Balsamic: An aged wine vinegar from Modena, Italy, balsamic vinegar is made from the cooked juice of grapes and aged for a minimum of twelve years in wooden casks. It is very rare and expensive. It must be approved by the Italian government and sold in specially marked bottles with the seal and designation "Aceto Balsamico Traditionale." Inexpensive versions of balsamic vinegar are fortified with caramelized sugar, herbs, and other flavorings. Unless you are paying a small fortune for a bottle, you are getting the stuff with the caramelized sugar, but that's OK too.

Black: Black vinegar has a very low acid content and is blended with rice, sugar, and spices. It is usually used in Chinese and Pacific Rim cuisines. You can find it in Asian grocery stores.

Cane: Cane vinegar is fermented from sugar cane extract and water, and has a very low acid content. It is used in Cajun and Philippine cuisines.

Champagne: Champagne vinegar is made from champagne grapes and is often used to make fruit vinegars. It can have two different tastes, either delicate or very sharp.

Cider: Cider vinegar is fermented apple juice or cider. It works well in tomato-based sauces.

Malt: Malt vinegar is made using a sugar infusion of malted barley.

Red wine: Red wine vinegar is created from hearty red wines.

Rice: Rice vinegar is made with rice and sugar. It is used in Asian cuisines.

Sherry: Sherry vinegar is usually a product of Spain. It is aged in wooden casks and has a fine mellow flavor.

White distilled: White vinegar is naturally fermented in a carefully controlled environment and then distilled. It has the sharpest, strongest flavor of all the vinegars.

White wine: White wine vinegar can range from mellow to sharp, depending on the base wine used.

In addition to the basic types of vinegar, there are flavored vinegars, of which raspberry vinegar is the most popular. To make a flavored vinegar, you start with a commercial vinegar, heat it along with something to add a flavor, and let it steep like a tea. Then strain the vinegar, and bottle it. It's a good idea to stick a fresh sprig of the herb, or a piece of the fruit or vegetable you used for flavoring, into the strained and bottled vinegar to help identify its flavor at a glance. Flavored vinegars, placed in clean jars and tightly capped, will keep as long as a year if stored in a cool, dark place or in the refrigerator. Using flavored vinegars in your marinades, mops, and sauces can add an extra level of zest to your barbecue.

Fresh Raspberry Vinegar

Raspberry vinegar is probably the most popular flavored vinegar. It's used more in salad dressing than barbecue, but it might turn out to be your secret sauce ingredient. You never know. This particular version is very sweet—almost a sweet-and-sour vinegar.

Makes about 2 quarts

6   cups fresh raspberries
4   cups white or white wine vinegar
4   cups cane sugar

Wash the berries, and place them in a nonreactive bowl. Mash them thoroughly, and blend in the vinegar. Cover tightly with a nonreactive lid or plastic wrap secured with a rubber band, and let the mixture rest for 2 to 3 days in a cool, dry place.

Strain the mixture into a nonreactive saucepan, pressing the berries with the back of a spoon to extract as much juice as possible. Add the sugar, and blend it in. Cook the mixture over medium heat, stirring constantly. Bring it to a boil, reduce the heat to low, and cook, still stirring constantly, for 5 minutes. Pour the vinegar into clean bottles or jars with nonreactive lids. Close them tightly.

The flavor of the vinegar will be stronger if it is allowed to sit for a few weeks before using. Store it in the refrigerator.

■ How to Use It: This vinegar is wonderful in salad dressings and marinades.

Raspberry Red Wine Vinegar

Unlike the previous recipe, this vinegar is very tart in flavor. It requires IQF (individually quick frozen) raspberries—they are the ones that don't completely disintegrate when thawed.

Makes about 1 quart

2   10-ounce packages unsweetened frozen raspberries, thawed
4   cups red wine vinegar

Gently rinse the frozen raspberries with cold water, and drain. Thaw completely, then drain again, reserving the juice for another use.

Place the drained berries in a nonreactive saucepan, and blend in the vinegar. Let the mixture sit, uncovered, for 8 hours. Then bring it to a boil over medium-high heat, and boil for 3 to 5 minutes. Let the mixture cool. Strain it through a fine mesh, discarding the solids.

Pour the vinegar into clean bottles or jars with nonreactive lids and close them tightly. Store the vinegar in a cool, dark place for 2 to 3 weeks before using.

■ **How to Use It:** Use this vinegar in salad dressings and marinades.

Tarragon Vinegar

Tarragon is usually associated with vinegar and fish. Its anise-like character is particularly suited to both. With so seductive and satisfying a flavor, tarragon really deserves a wider role in the kitchen.

Makes about 1 quart

4   ounces fresh tarragon
1   quart white wine vinegar

Wash the tarragon, and pat it dry with a paper towel. Put about 3 ounces of the tarragon in a nonreactive saucepan with the vinegar, and bring to a boil. Remove from the heat, cover, and let sit overnight. Refrigerate the leftover tarragon.

Put the remaining fresh tarragon in clean bottles with nonreactive lids. Strain the vinegar through a fine mesh to remove the cooked tarragon. Bring the strained vinegar mixture to a boil. Pour the hot vinegar into the clean bottles, cover tightly, and let sit for 3 weeks before using. Store the vinegar in the refrigerator.

■ **How to Use It:** Use this vinegar in salad dressings and in marinades for chicken or pork.

Garlic Vinegar

Since garlic goes well with so many different foods, garlic vinegar is one of the most versatile flavored vinegars.

Makes about 1 quart

1   large bulb of garlic
1   quart white wine vinegar

Peel the garlic cloves, and divide them into two piles. Smash half of the garlic cloves, and put them into a nonreactive saucepan with the vinegar. Bring to a boil over medium-high heat, reduce the heat to low, and simmer for 30 minutes. Cover the saucepan, and remove it from the heat. Let the mixture sit overnight.

The next day, strain the mixture through a fine mesh to remove the garlic. Divide the fresh garlic among clean bottles or jars with nonreactive lids.

Bring the vinegar mixture to a boil, pour it into the bottles, cap tightly, and let the vinegar sit for 1 to 2 weeks before using it. Store the vinegar in a cool, dark place.

■ **Variation:** Garlic-Basil Vinegar. Gently wash 3 ounces of fresh basil leaves, put them on a cookie sheet lined with paper towels, and let them dry for 2 to 3 days. Really—the leaves must be bone-dry. Then add two thirds of the dried leaves to the smashed garlic and vinegar solution, saving the rest of the leaves. Proceed as directed. Discard the cooked basil leaves along with the cooked garlic. Add the remaining basil to the bottles along with the fresh garlic when bottling.

Jalapeño Pepper Vinegar

If you like the flavor of jalapeños, this is a good way to get a little kick in your barbecue. The heat of this vinegar is determined by how many peppers you use and how hot they are—vary it according to your taste.

Makes about 1 quart

- 12 jalapeños
- 1 quart white vinegar
- ½ cup sugar
- ¼ cup sliced onion
- 2 tablespoons vegetable oil
- 6 to 8 garlic cloves, crushed
- 1 teaspoon black peppercorns, crushed
- ½ teaspoon dried oregano

With a sharp-pointed knife, cut slits in the jalapeños.

Combine all of the ingredients in a nonreactive saucepan, and bring to a boil. Reduce the heat, and simmer for 5 to 7 minutes. Cover, and let the mixture cool to room temperature. Pour the mixture into clean bottles or jars with nonreactive lids, dividing the peppers, garlic, and peppercorns among the bottles, and close tightly.

This vinegar has fuller flavor, and its heat level intensifies, if it is allowed to sit for 2 weeks before using. Store it in the refrigerator. After 2 weeks, strain the vinegar through a fine mesh to remove the solids. Return it to clean jars and cap with nonreactive lids. Store it in the refrigerator.

■ How to Use It: Use this vinegar in sauces and marinades when extra heat is desired.

2

Barbecue Seasonings and Rubs

Barbecue seasonings and rubs are, for the most part, dry ingredients that can be rubbed or sprinkled on meat or vegetables before cooking to enhance their flavor when grilled, smoked, or barbecued. Dry rubs are dry marinades. The reason most pitmasters prefer rubs over marinades is that you can't get a good crust on meat with a marinade, but you do with a rub. To me, the word rub is a misnomer, because I believe that if you rub the seasoning into the meat, it can clog the pores of the meat. That's why I recommend that you sprinkle a rub on as if you were seasoning a dish heavily with salt and pepper.

People ask me what I think is the most important aspect of barbecue: the rub, cooker, smoker, fire, wood, charcoal, meat, what? All things being equal, my answer is without a doubt the rub or barbecue seasoning! If you have a good rub, your chances of being the neighborhood Barbecue King, or this year's big winner in barbecue competitions, are very good. The next thing people usually want to know is what's in my rub and whether I'll give out the recipe. My answer is, sure, you can have what's in my rub, but I won't give you the proportions. My rub consists of sugar, salt, paprika, chili powder, pepper, and other spices.

Instead of giving you my rub recipe, I think you will benefit more if I teach you how to develop your own rub, so that's what the Master Class is all about: how to create your own championship rub.

And for those of you who are too lazy to construct your own rub, or who are simply interested in trying out some tried-and-true rubs, there are eighteen more recipes, including some that have no salt and some that have no sugar. Even though I generally recommend a balanced approach for building a rub, you can break all the rules and still make a good rub.

Rubs that contain no sugar are your best bet for grilling. The sugar in most rubs will blacken and caramelize over the high heat of a direct flame—you've seen it happen when you've applied the barbecue sauce too early in the cooking. The same thing will happen with rubs—unless you are using indirect heat, which is what barbecuing is all about.

Barbecue pastes, or wet rubs, are not very common anymore, but they are on the comeback trail. Up until last year, I had seen only about five or six people using wet rubs in competition rather than dry rubs or marinades. Then last year, more than seventy-five different teams on the barbecue contest circuit used a wet rub. A wet rub is really a combination of a dry rub and a marinade—it's a paste you apply to your meat before barbecuing.

Master Class: Constructing a Championship Rub

STEP ONE: OBSERVE THE COMPETITION AND THE MASTERS.

Beg, borrow, buy, or steal every recipe or label that shows the ingredients of every rub and/or barbecue seasoning that you can find. Grocery and spice stores are a good place to start. There are a lot of recipes in cookbooks, too, so look there. The best place to get ideas is at barbecue competitions, by asking the

The Baron's K.C. BBQ Seasoning & Rub	Cain's Barbecue Spice	K.C. Rib Doctor Barbecue Rub
salt	sugar	sugar
sugar	chile pepper	salt
paprika	paprika	spices
chili seasoning	salt	paprika
pepper	arrowroot starch	pepper
garlic	coriander	dehydrated onion
celery	celery seed	dehydrated garlic
other spices	garlic	hickory smoke
	red pepper	flavor
	MSG	natural flavors
	silicon dioxide	less than 2%
	pyroligneous acid	calcium cyclicate
	(artificial smoke flavor)	
	citric acid	

competitors. Listen to what they are saying, and be observant of the spices around their barbecue space.

STEP TWO: MAKE A LIST OF THE STANDARD INGREDIENTS.

List every ingredient on each label or recipe side by side as shown below. If you don't know what they are, find out!

STEP THREE: COMPARE ALL OF THE INGREDIENTS OF EACH RUB.

Remember that the first ingredient listed on a label occurs in the greatest proportion. The ingredients are listed in decreasing amounts. In our examples, the first rub has more salt than sugar. The next two rubs have more sugar than salt. All of the commercial rubs use paprika, and two of the six use chili pepper or chili seasoning. Make this comparison of each of the ingredients. If you come across an ingredient that you don't

Soul Chef–Chicago Spicy BBQ Seasoning	Basic Texas Rub	Johnny's Pork & Chicken Seasoning
soy flour	salt	salt
sugar, dextrose	paprika	paprika
salt	black pepper	dehydrated garlic
spices		dehydrated onion
citric acid		spices
onion powder		sage
garlic powder		marjoram
natural smoke flavor		thyme
extract of paprika		MSG
silica gel		disodium inosinate
not more than 2% disodium guanylate		

recognize, find out about it. (Call a spice company.) Then compare the ingredients in two or three rub or seasoning recipes you find in cookbooks, or get them from other successful barbecuers, and see what they have in common. With several rub labels and two or three recipes, you should be ready to construct your championship seasoning or rub.

STEP FOUR: CONSTRUCT *YOUR* CHAMPIONSHIP RUB.

Now it's time to experiment and put your newly acquired knowledge of spices to work. The rub from the recipe you are going to construct will weigh anywhere from 18 to 24 ounces (or will measure 2¼ to 3 cups). It's best to start with a small batch, so that if you are not satisfied with the results, you can pitch it in the trash and not be out a lot of money.

In analyzing the above seasonings, you will find that the two main ingredients are *salt* and *sugar*. We will start with equal amounts of each in this example, using 1 cup of salt and 1 cup of sugar, but you can use any amount that you desire. A key point to keep in mind is that you do not want any of the flavors you choose to dominate or overpower.

Of the salts that you have to choose from, I think the major portion of your salt should be seasoned salt. In this case, it would be ½ cup. The reason I suggest this is that most commercial seasoned salts are proven flavor enhancers, and I feel that is a plus for someone just starting. The rest of the salt can be a combination of any other salts, up to ½ cup. In general, I recommend using non-iodized salt, because iodized salt can leave streaks or spots on your meat.

The next part of the rub is the sugar, which is much more controversial than salt, mainly because a lot of the favorite brands of smoked meats are "brown sugar cured." Brown sugar has great flavor (a light molasses flavor), but it is high in moisture and difficult to work with because it clumps. I recommend cane sugar or white sugar, but not beet sugar. It doesn't have the flavor or flavor-enhancing abilities that cane sugar has. Another thing to keep in mind when developing your rub is that the granules should remain similar in size so that they'll blend well and not separate. If you want to use brown sugar, you can dry it by placing it on a cookie sheet, spreading it out as evenly as possible, and letting it air-dry, turning and mixing it every 2 to 3 hours until it is dry. Then, you'll need to sift it. One word of caution: it won't be as tasty as it was when it was damp.

Sugars: 1 cup
Salts: 1 cup
Balance the sugars and salts

Sugars	*Salts*	
white sugar: cane and beet	seasoned salt	hickory salt*
brown sugar: light and dark	garlic salt	smoked salt*
corn sugar	celery salt	charcoal salt*
maple sugar	onion salt	kosher salt**
date sugar	sea salt**	plain/table salt

---

* These flavored salts generally should not be used in your rub. Your smoke flavor should come directly from the smoke.
** I don't recommend using these salts in a rub because the granules are usually too large, but there are some sea salts that have the same size granules as regular salt.

Next, pour the sugars and salts into a sifter that is set over a 3 to 4 quart, nonreactive bowl—but don't sift.

What is the next most predominant spice? Paprika! Paprika is a very mild member of the genus *Capsicum* and is used more for color than seasoning. I suggest ⅓ to ½ cup for proper balance. By balance, I mean it will have good color and make your barbecue look ever so good. Add it to the sugars and salts in the sifter, and add the other spices as well.

Paprika: ⅓ to ½ cup

The next two main ingredients are chili powder or chili seasoning and black pepper. Chili powder and chili seasoning are the same thing. They are both a ground chile pepper, or a blend of ground chile peppers, with cumin, garlic, oregano, and other spices. In your rub construction, I suggest a balance between chili powder and pepper. If you use 2 tablespoons of chili powder, use 2 tablespoons of pepper. This recipe can handle 2 to 4 tablespoons (⅛ to ¼ cup) each of chili powder or seasoning and black pepper.

Chili powder or seasoning: 2 to 4 tablespoons
Black pepper: 2 to 4 tablespoons
Balance the chili seasoning and pepper

When you analyze the rest of the ingredients, none really sticks out or dominates, so the next ingredient is "other spices."

If you followed instructions, you now have your "basic rub" for your championship seasoning. Now is when you put your signature on it—or better, in it!

For your signature, pick two to four spices that you think will enhance your barbecue, or just pick your favorite spices. Use a teaspoon or less of each spice you pick, and add your choices to the basic rub in the sifter.

Other spices: Use 1 teaspoon or less

Signature Spices

allspice
anise
barbecue spice
basil
bay leaf, whole or
    powdered
caraway seeds
cayenne
celery seeds, whole
    or ground
chervil
chives
cilantro
cinnamon
citric acid
cloves
coriander

crushed red pepper
cumin
curry powder
dill
fennel
garlic, granulated
    or powdered
ginger
horseradish powder
jalapeño powder
lemon pepper
lemon powder
lemon zest
mace
marjoram
mint
MSG

dry mustard
nutmeg
onion, granulated
    or powdered
orange zest
oregano
parsley
rosemary
sage, ground or
    rubbed
savory
tarragon
thyme
turmeric
white pepper

Less Common Signature Spices

beet powder
brandy pepper
carrot powder

soy sauce powder
tomato powder
vanilla powder

vinegar powder
Worcestershire
    powder

Run the mixture through the sifter.

Congratulations! You have just blended an all-purpose rub. Taste it and see what you think. It could taste great or it could taste not so great. Don't be too critical. The only true test of a rub is to cook with it.

> To get accurate measures when making barbecue seasonings, rubs, and sauces, overfill the measuring cup and level with the back side of a knife. It is assumed that all tablespoons, teaspoons, and cups are level, not heaping.

STEP FIVE: USE THE RUB.

If you read the section on mustards, you know that I consider using mustard with a rub to be one of my secrets to success. First, paint the meat with a mustard or mustard sauce. Then sprinkle—don't rub—the rub onto the meat. Some people prefer to let the rub marinate the meat for a while. I normally don't let it marinate for any length of time; I just season it with the rub, and put it on my pit. Then I cook the meat over indirect heat.

Sample Master Class Barbecue Rub

If you constructed a rub according to the Master Class, it might look something like this one.

Makes about 3 cups

1 cup cane sugar
¼ cup seasoned salt
¼ cup garlic salt
¼ cup celery salt
¼ cup onion salt
½ cup paprika
3 tablespoons chili powder
2 tablespoons black pepper
1 tablespoon lemon pepper
2 teaspoons ground sage
1 teaspoon dry mustard powder
½ teaspoon ground thyme
½ teaspoon cayenne

Rubs on Marinated Meat
Marinated meat should be blotted with paper towels before sprinkling on your rub or seasoning.

Combine all of the ingredients in a sifter, and sift to blend well. Store in an airtight jar in the refrigerator for 2 to 3 weeks or in the freezer for up to 6 months.

■ **How to Use It:** This is a good all-purpose rub for beef, lamb, pork, chicken, or fish. Sprinkle it on heavily, and cook over indirect heat.

Sweet Rub

This rub breaks all the rules and contains lots of sugar. It definitely should not be used for grilled foods.

Makes about 3 1/2 cups

2 cups cane sugar
1 cup Master Barbecue Spice (page 21)
½ cup seasoned salt

1   teaspoon ground allspice
½   teaspoon ground ginger
¼   teaspoon ground cloves

Combine all of the ingredients in a sifter, and sift to blend well. Store in an airtight jar in the refrigerator for 2 to 3 weeks or in the freezer for up to 6 months.

■ **How to Use It:** This rub is exceptional on chicken and ribs. Sprinkle it on heavily, and cook over indirect heat. Keep a watchful eye out for charring or scorching. Move the meat to a cooler spot if it looks like it might burn.

■ **Variation:** Sweet and hot is how many people like it. Add 2 tablespoons black pepper, 1 tablespoon ground dried New Mexico chiles, 1 tablespoon ground dried jalapeño, and 1 teaspoon ground dried habanero chile.

A Basic Texas Barbecue Rub

It doesn't get any simpler than this. This rub is a good starting point for those who want to see what different spices do or how they enhance the meat they are on. Cook with this rub. The next time, add some chili seasoning, the next time, some garlic, and so on, until you find the right combination for you.

Makes 3/4 cup

¼   cup salt
¼   cup paprika
¼   cup black pepper

Mix together in a bowl. Store in an airtight jar in the refrigerator for 2 to 3 weeks or in the freezer for up to 6 months.

■ **How to Use It:** Use this rub for beef, lamb, pork, chicken, or fish. Sprinkle it on heavily. This rub can be used on both grilled meats and barbecue cooked over indirect heat because of the absence of sugar in the rub.

Sugarless Texas Sprinkle Barbecue Rub

A smooth blend of spices, with no sugar. A tablespoon of cayenne gives this rub a good wallop of heat.

Makes about 1 cup

⅓ cup salt
¼ cup paprika
3   tablespoons chili powder
2   tablespoons black pepper
1   tablespoon ground cumin
1   tablespoon garlic powder
1   tablespoon cayenne

Combine all of the ingredients in a sifter, and sift to blend well. Store in an airtight jar in the refrigerator for 2 to 3 weeks or in the freezer for up to 6 months.

■ **How to Use It:** Sprinkle this rub very heavily on your brisket, ribs, pork, chicken, or fish. This rub can be used on both grilled meats and barbecue cooked over indirect heat because of the absence of sugar in the rub.

Breaking the Rules

Once I had a fellow from Ethiopia come to one of my classes. They use a lot of spices in Ethiopian cooking. Well, this fellow had about twenty different ingredients in his rub. I doubted that the rub would have any good flavor at all; it was excessive. Darned if his ribs didn't turn out to be the best in the class.

Creole Seasoning and Barbecue Rub

This is considered a creole seasoning because of the capsicums, garlic, and black pepper.

Makes about 1 cup

½ cup salt
2 tablespoons cane sugar
2 tablespoons paprika
1 tablespoon black pepper
2 teaspoons cayenne
1 teaspoon garlic powder
¼ teaspoon MSG (optional)

Combine all of the ingredients in a sifter, and sift to blend well. Store in an airtight jar in the refrigerator for 2 to 3 weeks or in the freezer for up to 6 months.

■ **How to Use It:** You can use this stuff just like salt and sprinkle it on just about any food to which you want to give a little creole lift. Or, use it as a rub—it's particularly good on ribs.

■ **Variation:** Adding a teaspoon of thyme, ground parsley, and/or ground bay leaf to this seasoning keeps with the theme and adds some nice herb flavors.

Zesty No-Salt Herbal Rub

Do you have to go without barbecue if your doctor puts you on a no-salt diet? No way. This is a good rub and a good salt substitute, too.

Makes about 2 cups

1¼ cups cane sugar
¼ cup chili powder
1 tablespoon granulated garlic
1 tablespoon granulated onion
2 teaspoons dried ground New Mexico chiles
2 teaspoons black pepper
2 teaspoons dried dill weed
2 teaspoons lemon powder*
2 teaspoons rubbed sage
1 teaspoon ground cumin
1 teaspoon ground celery seed
1 teaspoon dried basil
1 teaspoon dried marjoram
1 teaspoon dry mustard powder
1 teaspoon dried parsley flakes
1 teaspoon crushed dried rosemary
1 teaspoon cayenne

Combine all of the ingredients in a sifter, and sift to blend well. Store in an airtight jar in the refrigerator for 2 to 3 weeks or in the freezer for up to 6 months.

■ **How to Use It:** I have used this rub successfully in competition on ribs and chicken. I have also used it as a salt substitute when I've cooked for people who are on salt-restricted diets. This rub is excellent on grilled vegetables, such as zucchini, onions, and eggplant.

*****Note:** See page 30 for information on lemon powder.

Bill's Beef Power Rub

One of my students, Bill Stockley, developed this rub. He has won seven blue ribbons with it in competition. You'll probably find it a winner yourself!

Makes about 2³/4 cups

- 1 cup cane sugar
- 1 cup garlic salt
- ½ cup paprika
- 3 tablespoons black pepper
- 2 tablespoons chili powder
- 1 tablespoon powdered beef base*
- 1 teaspoon ground ginger
- 1 teaspoon onion powder
- 1 teaspoon ground coriander
- 1 teaspoon cayenne

Combine all of the ingredients in a sifter, and sift to blend well. Store in an airtight jar in the refrigerator for 2 to 3 weeks or in the freezer for up to 6 months.

■ **How to Use It:** Use this rub on any beef cut. Sprinkle it on heavily, and cook over indirect heat.

*****Note:** Powdered beef base is a powdered form of the same substance beef bouillon cubes or granules are made of. If you cannot find powdered beef base, make it yourself by grinding bouillon granules fine in a spice grinder.

Old Mill Barbecue Pork Rub

This recipe comes from one of the country's foremost experts on traditional barbecue, Mason Steinberg. If you ever get a chance to talk barbecue with him at the Old Mill Barbecue in Omaha, Nebraska, expect to spend some enjoyable time. This rub is considered an "advanced" rub because it uses such uncommon ingredients as vinegar powder and Worcestershire powder. For sources of these hard-to-find ingredients, check the listings under Spices and Seasonings in the Resources.

Makes about 3 cups

1   cup dark brown sugar
1   cup celery salt
½   cup paprika
2½ tablespoons chili powder
2   tablespoons black pepper
2   tablespoons vinegar or citric acid powder
1   tablespoon Worcestershire powder
1   tablespoon ground sage
1   teaspoon garlic powder
1   teaspoon crushed red pepper
1   teaspoon ground allspice
1   teaspoon dry mustard powder
½   teaspoon ground cinnamon

Combine all of the ingredients in a sifter, and sift to blend well. Store in an airtight jar in the refrigerator for 2 to 3 weeks or in the freezer for up to 6 months.

■ **How to Use It:** Use this rub for pork shoulder or ribs. Sprinkle it on heavily, and cook over indirect heat.

Free-range chickens are allowed to forage for food outside their pen. Organic chickens are raised on chemical-free land and fed chemical-free grain. A kosher chicken is one that is killed according to the Jewish dietary laws under the supervision of a rabbi.

Steve's Hot Chicken Rub

This recipe is from my BBQ sidekick Steve Holbrook, who helped design and build my first big barbecue rig—a smoker— on wheels. One year we each had our own team and went head to head at various competitions, especially in the chicken category. If he came in third, I would come in second. If he came in second, I would come in first. Then came the American Royal, and Steve came first with best chicken overall. I didn't even place in that one. This rub is the one he developed.

Makes about 3 cups

1   cup cane sugar
½   cup onion salt
½   cup garlic salt
½   cup paprika
2   tablespoons chili powder
1   tablespoon black pepper
1   tablespoon lemon pepper
1   tablespoon cayenne
1   tablespoon rubbed sage
1   tablespoon dried basil
1   teaspoon crushed dried rosemary

Combine all of the ingredients in a sifter, and sift to blend well. Store in an airtight jar in the refrigerator for 2 to 3 weeks or in the freezer for up to 6 months.

■ **How to Use It:** Use this rub for chicken parts or for whole chicken. Sprinkle it on heavily, and cook over indirect heat. You can also use it as a seasoning for grilled chicken or fish.

Mitch's Fantastic Barbecue Rub

Mitch's rub is fantastic because it goes with almost everything, from brisket to chicken to ribs. Mitch is one of those sneaky little barbecuers who will never give up a recipe—so I wagered my recipe against his that Jim Erickson and I could tell him eighty percent of what he had in his recipe. Here it is, and his jaw is still dragging on the ground.

Makes about 2³/4 cups

- ¾ cup cane sugar
- ¼ cup light brown sugar
- 6 tablespoons celery salt
- ¼ cup seasoned salt
- ¼ cup onion salt
- 2 tablespoons garlic salt
- ⅓ cup paprika
- 2 tablespoons chili powder
- 2 tablespoons black pepper
- 1 tablespoon cayenne
- 1 teaspoon ground allspice
- 1 teaspoon MSG (optional)
- ½ teaspoon ground cloves
- ½ teaspoon ground bay leaf

Combine all of the ingredients in a sifter, and sift to blend well. Store in an airtight jar in the refrigerator for 2 to 3 weeks or in the freezer for up to 6 months.

■ **How to Use It:** Use this rub on beef, lamb, pork, chicken, or fish. Sprinkle it on heavily, and cook over indirect heat.

Mikey's Half-Cup Rub

It's true that Mikey will eat anything, and it is also true that he will concoct almost anything. Mikey says that if you don't use at least a half a cup of his rub every time you use it, you're not using enough! Don't be shy about stealing some of the kids' lime-flavored Kool-Aid—the savory ingredients in the rub will tone down the sweetness of the drink mix.

Makes about 3 cups

½ cup cane sugar
½ cup maple sugar
½ cup garlic salt
½ cup onion salt
½ cup paprika
2 tablespoons lemon pepper
2 tablespoons granulated garlic
1 tablespoon lime powder (e.g., lime-flavored Kool-Aid or Country Time limeade)
1 tablespoon dried parsley flakes
1 teaspoon cayenne
1 teaspoon ground ginger
1 teaspoon ground cinnamon
½ teaspoon ground anise

Combine all of the ingredients in a sifter, and sift to blend well. Store in an airtight jar in the refrigerator for 2 to 3 weeks or in the freezer for up to 6 months.

■ **How to Use It:** This rub is good on any cut of fish, chicken, or pork. I use it when I grill country-style pork ribs; it gives the ribs a glaze that's sweet with a hot and spicy kick.

■ **Variation:** For an orange flavor, instead of the lemon-and-lime, replace the lemon pepper with simple black pepper and the lime powder with orange powder or 2 tablespoons minced orange peel.

Doctor Dolan's Barbecue Rub

All the Doc will say is that this will fix what ails your barbecue.

Makes about 2³/4 cups

- ½ cup dark brown sugar*
- ½ cup cane sugar
- ½ cup garlic salt
- ¼ cup onion salt
- 3 tablespoons salt
- 1 tablespoon celery salt
- ¼ cup chili powder
- ¼ cup paprika
- 3 tablespoons black pepper
- 1 tablespoon cayenne
- 2 teaspoons MSG (optional)
- ½ teaspoon ground allspice
- ½ teaspoon dried oregano
- ½ teaspoon dried summer savory

Combine all of the ingredients in a sifter, and sift to blend well. Store in an airtight jar in the refrigerator for 2 to 3 weeks or in the freezer for up to 6 months.

■ **How to Use It:** This rub really shines on brisket and pork shoulder, but you can use it for any cut of beef, lamb, pork, chicken, or fish. Sprinkle it on heavily, and cook over indirect heat.

*Note: The brown sugar should be dried before using it in the spice rub. Place it on a cookie sheet, spreading it out as evenly as possible, and let it air-dry, stirring and turning it every 2 to 3 hours until it is dry. When it's dry, you will need to sift it.

Andy's Rub

Andy was a student who didn't follow my instructions for developing a rub, and he ended up with the best ribs of all in a class of twenty-two students. Here is his rub.

Makes about 2½ cups

- 1 cup cane sugar
- ½ cup seasoned salt
- 3 tablespoons garlic salt
- 3 tablespoons celery salt
- 2 tablespoons onion salt
- ⅓ cup paprika
- 2 tablespoons black pepper
- 1 tablespoon lemon pepper
- 1 teaspoon ground celery seed
- 1 teaspoon dry mustard powder
- 1 teaspoon ground thyme
- ½ teaspoon ground allspice
- ½ teaspoon cayenne
- ½ teaspoon dried chives

Combine all of the ingredients except the chives in a sifter, and sift to blend. Crumble the chives into tiny pieces, and mix in well. Store in an airtight jar in the refrigerator for 2 to 3 weeks or in the freezer for up to 6 months.

■ **How to Use It:** This rub is supreme on baby back ribs! Sprinkle it on the ribs heavily, and cook over indirect heat.

A Power Rub

Earlier in this chapter, I wrote that hickory salt doesn't belong in a rub, that you should get your smoke flavor from the fire. Thwack. The sound of another rule being broken. This recipe is called a "Power Rub" because the first time it was used it took a first place ribbon in the chicken category, a second in ribs, a second in brisket, a third in pork shoulder, as well as reserve grand champion. So it was thrown back into my face as an "I told you so" recipe. I still think hickory salt has no place in a rub. But if you want to use it, this recipe proves you can, and that you can be successful doing it!

Makes about 3 cups

¾ cup Master Barbecue Spice (see page 21)
½ cup seasoned salt
½ cup brown sugar*
½ cup cane sugar
⅓ cup paprika
¼ cup celery salt
2 tablespoons hickory salt
2 tablespoons black pepper
2 teaspoons celery seeds
1 teaspoon garlic powder
1 teaspoon cayenne
¼ teaspoon MSG (optional)

Combine all of the ingredients in a sifter, and sift to blend well. Store in an airtight jar in the refrigerator for 2 to 3 weeks or in the freezer for up to 6 months.

■ **How to Use It:** This is a good all-purpose rub for any cut of beef, pork, lamb, chicken, or fish. Sprinkle it on heavily, and cook over indirect heat.

■ **Variation:** For a hotter rub, you can add 1 to 2 tablespoons of ground dried jalapeño or crushed red pepper.

***Note:** The brown sugar should be dried before using it in the spice rub. Place it on a cookie sheet, spreading it out as evenly as possible, and let it air-dry, stirring and turning it every 2 to 3 hours until it is dry. When it's dry, you will need to sift it.

Monty's Voo-Doo Rub

Monty's Voo-Doo Barbecue Team is legendary around barbecue competitions, but it's not because of their barbecue, it is because of the great parties they throw. Even without the party, this is still a good rub.

Makes about 2³/4 cups

    1   cup cane sugar
    ½   cup seasoned salt
    ¼   cup garlic salt
    2   tablespoons celery salt
    2   tablespoons onion salt
    ½   cup paprika
    1   tablespoon black pepper
    1   tablespoon chili powder
    1   tablespoon dry mustard powder
    1   teaspoon garlic powder
    ½   teaspoon cayenne
    ½   teaspoon MSG (optional)

Combine all of the ingredients in a sifter, and sift to blend well. Store in an airtight jar in the refrigerator for 2 to 3 weeks or in the freezer for up to 6 months.

■ **How to Use It:** This is a good all-purpose rub for any cut of beef, pork, lamb, chicken, or fish. Sprinkle it on heavily, and cook over indirect heat.

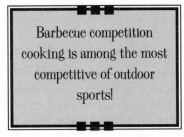

Barbecue competition cooking is among the most competitive of outdoor sports!

Cajun Barbecue Rub

Cajun cooking is appreciated for its complex spice blends and soul-searing heat. This rub truly delivers on flavor, without being excessively hot.

Makes about 3 cups

½ cup dark brown sugar*
½ cup cane sugar
½ cup seasoned salt
¼ cup Cajun Spice Blend (page 24)
2 tablespoons garlic salt
1 tablespoon onion salt
1 tablespoon celery salt
½ cup paprika
2 tablespoons chili powder
2 tablespoons black pepper
2 tablespoons dry mustard powder
1 tablespoon cayenne
1 teaspoon garlic powder
1 teaspoon ground marjoram
½ teaspoon ground thyme
½ teaspoon ground cumin
½ teaspoon ground allspice
½ teaspoon MSG (optional)

Combine all of the ingredients in a sifter, and sift to blend well. Store in an airtight jar in the refrigerator for 2 to 3 weeks or in the freezer for up to 6 months.

■ **How to Use It:** This Cajun rub is great on shrimp, catfish, eel, and frog's legs. Without the brown and white sugar, you can use it as a seasoning mix for your next gumbo or jambalaya.

*Note: The brown sugar should be dried before using it in the spice rub. Place it on a cookie sheet, spreading it out as evenly as possible, and let it air-dry, stirring and turning it every 2 to 3 hours until it is dry. When it's dry, you will need to sift it.

Tom's Barbecue Rub

This recipe is from my good friend Tommy Byron, who competes in the Memphis in May World Barbecue Contest every year. He is legendary for several things, including his Cajun Breakfast Potatoes and his barbecue in the Memphis contest. Tom is a perfect example of someone who makes good barbecue, and knows it, but the judges can't seem to figure it out. We don't call Tommy "0 and 13" for nothing!

Makes about 3 cups

½ cup cane sugar
½ cup dark brown sugar*
⅓ cup seasoned salt
⅓ cup garlic salt
⅓ cup onion salt
½ cup paprika
2 tablespoons chili powder
2 tablespoons black pepper
2 tablespoons dry mustard powder
2 tablespoons rubbed sage
1 teaspoon ground ginger
1 teaspoon ground thyme
1 teaspoon cayenne
½ teaspoon ground nutmeg

Combine all of the ingredients in a sifter, and sift to blend well. Store in an airtight jar in the refrigerator for 2 to 3 weeks or in the freezer for up to 6 months.

■ **How to Use It:** This is a good all-purpose rub to use on any cut of beef, pork, lamb, or chicken. Sprinkle it on heavily, and cook over indirect heat.

*Note: The brown sugar should be dried before using in the spice rub. Place it on a cookie sheet, spreading it out as evenly as possible, and let it air-dry, stirring and turning it every 2 to 3 hours until it is dry. When it's dry, you will need to sift it.

Basic Wet Rub

When I was in South Korea, teaching Midwestern barbecue to a group of chefs in the hotel and restaurant industry, I ran into a brick wall with respect to spices. In the four hotel kitchens I worked in, they had very few or no dried spices. So I developed this wet rub to use on beef and pork.

Makes about 1⅓ cups

- 1 cup lard or solid vegetable shortening
- 2 tablespoons brown sugar
- 1 tablespoon paprika
- 1 teaspoon onion powder or 1 tablespoon grated onion
- ½ teaspoon cayenne
- 2 tablespoons fresh lemon juice
- 2 tablespoons Worcestershire sauce
- 1 teaspoon garlic salt or 1 garlic clove, pressed, plus
- ½ teaspoon salt

In a mixing bowl, cream the lard, sugar, paprika, onion, and cayenne. In a separate bowl, combine the lemon juice, Worcestershire sauce, and garlic salt, and blend until the salt has dissolved. Add slowly to the lard mixture. Blend thoroughly. Use immediately.

■ **How to Use It:** Massage the paste into any cut of beef or pork. Cook over indirect heat.

Spicy Orange Wet Rub

As far as I'm concerned, this wet rub on a barbecued duck beats duck à l'orange any day.

Makes about 1 1/4 cups

½ cup butter (1 stick), softened
½ cup light brown sugar
¼ cup orange juice concentrate
2 teaspoons minced orange zest
½ teaspoon ground mace
½ teaspoon ground allspice
½ teaspoon salt
¼ teaspoon cayenne

Combine the butter and brown sugar in a mixing bowl. Beat with an electric mixer until smooth. Blend in the orange juice, add the spices, and mix well. Use immediately.

■ **How to Use It:** This paste is great to spread on poultry. When I was in South Korea, we rubbed it on duck. The recipe makes enough to coat two split chickens.

■ **Variation:** Spicy Lemon Barbecue Paste. Replace the orange juice concentrate with 2 tablespoons lemon juice, and replace the orange zest with lemon zest.

3
Marinades

The mysteries, mystiques, misbeliefs, and misinformation about marinades are unbelievable. You can get a different definition of "marinade" from anyone you ask or from any cookbook you read. I always like to start with the dictionary.

marinade *n.* A liquid mixture, usually of vinegar or wine and oil with various spices and herbs, in which meat, fowl, fish, and vegetables are soaked (marinated) before cooking. — marinade *tr. v.* To soak (food) in such a mixture; marinate.
marinate *v.* —*tr.* To soak (meat, for example) in a marinade. —*intr.* To become marinated.

The root of the word comes from "maritime," because the first marinades were brines for preserving fish. Brines use varying degrees of salt in water, and they aren't very popular today because of people's concern about the amount of salt in their diets. Basically, a marinade is made of an acid, like vinegar; a liquid, like oil, to replace moisture the acid draws out of the meat; and herbs or spices. Each of the three elements in your marinade has a specific job.

The acid works to soften the texture of the item marinated, which helps shorten the cooking process. Note that I did not say a marinade *tenderizes* the food—I said it *softens* the food. If you put a large piece of meat in a properly constructed marinade and marinate it for several hours, it will do what it's supposed to do: (1) give the meat flavor, (2) give it moisture from the oil, and (3) soften it. The acids will penetrate about ⅛ to ¼ of an inch, and sometimes a bit more. If a piece of meat sits in a marinade too long, the marinade doesn't really penetrate any deeper, the meat just becomes mushy.

Here's one example that I like to use to show people just how strong vinegar, or acid, really is. A friend of mine, a well-known barbecuer from the Kansas City area, learned this lesson the hard way. The rules of a major barbecue competition prohibited using steak in the beef category—you had to cook a chunk of beef, a roast. So my friend and his teammates, during one post-contest party, decided to barbecue a baron of beef, which is the whole round or back

> In competition, I would rather go up against a professional chef than a backyard barbecue cook! Why, you ask? The backyard barbecue cook works with a passion and love for what he is barbecuing. To many chefs, barbecue is just part of the job.

leg of a steer. It weighed about 43 pounds. My friend was accustomed to using a modest amount of a commercial marinade called Wicker's, which is 99 percent vinegar and 1 percent spices. He would inject the meat with Wicker's, and the result would be telltale streaks of gray lines and spices in the meat where he had injected it. He got the idea to use straight white vinegar with no spices in it to tenderize the baron of beef. They trimmed the baron and injected it with a *quart* of white vinegar, seasoned it with their rub, wrapped it with plastic wrap, put it in their cooler, and marinated it for 10 hours. Then they put it in their cooker and barbecued it for 10 hours. Gingerly they removed it from their cooker and let it rest about 30 minutes or so before the turn-in time. Then they came over to me and asked where they should cut to get the six perfect center-cut slices required to send to the judges. I showed them, and as they started to slice it, the whole 43-pound baron disintegrated—it just fell apart. It was a pile of dry mush that left nothing to be judged. Thank you, vinegar!

A lot of the time, you want the acid in a marinade to be a flavor carrier, too, which is why vinegar doesn't show up in every single recipe. Red wine is a strong acid that stands up well to beef. Lemon juice gives marinated foods a Mediterranean flavorprint; lime juice suggests Mexico or Southeast Asia, depending on the other spices used.

Oil in a marinade has the important job of replacing the moisture that the acids draw away. The oil can also be a flavoring agent, if you use one of the nut oils, like hazelnut or sesame oil, or a flavored oil, like the ones discussed in chapter 1.

Some marinades skip the oil and vinegar and just use yogurt or buttermilk. These dairy products hold down two jobs at once: providing both the acid for softening and the moisture.

The last element of a marinade is the mix of spices, seasonings, aromatics—in other words, the flavor. The signature of any marinade is in the spices. They are your creative license! I covered the spices, herbs, and other flavorings in chapter 1, so you know what I am talking about.

You'll notice that the recipes for the oil-vinegar-herb marinades sound a lot like salad dressing recipes. Well, they are similar, but the proportions are often different. You'll also see a lot of recipes for oriental-style marinades. An interesting trend that seems to be prevalent in competition barbecue today, especially for second- and third-year contestants, is what I call the "Oriental Phenomenon." This phenomenon occurs when a contestant sets his or her sights on new and mysterious cooking techniques, preparing teriyaki ribs, char siu pork, Korean beef, or some other exotic dish. The results are fun and delicious, and using the recipes expands your repertoire and improves your cooking abilities.

Marinade recipes can be used for mops and sauces and vice versa; feel free to experiment. The Brisket Marinade and Mop in chapter 4, made with beef stock, ketchup, lemon juice, Worcestershire sauce, and spices, is a good example. Set aside about 1 cup to be used as a mop while the brisket barbecues. You could even set aside a second cup to use as a dipping sauce.

Most marinades can be used interchangeably for beef, poultry, pork, and fish, but a marinade constructed specifically for beef may be more acidic than one for fish. If you are using a beef marinade for a more delicate meat, you may need to reduce the acid, especially if it tends to be overpowering, like red wine, or you may have to limit the marinating time. Generally, a piece of beef can marinate for 5 to 7 hours, pork and lamb for 3 to 5 hours, chicken for 2 to 4 hours, and fish for 1 to 2 hours.

Because marinades contain acidic ingredients, you should make them up in a nonreactive container—glass, ceramic, or stainless steel, never aluminum. If you are marinating a small piece of meat or fish, you can use a zippered plastic bag for the marinating.

Whatever you use to marinate, the food should be covered by the marinade and left in the refrigerator while it is marinating. If the meat isn't completely covered by the marinade, be sure to turn it over every 30 minutes or so.

Never reuse the marinade for any purpose. You don't want to risk giving everyone food poisoning from the bacteria that had a chance to breed in the liquid with the meat. Reuse includes basting or mopping with the marinade. It is best to set aside some marinade before the meat goes in.

You can use a marinade by itself or in conjunction with a rub. To use it with a rub, lift the meat out of the marinade and pat it dry with paper towels. Then apply the rub. This two-step process gives you the advantages of the marinade (flavoring and reduced cooking time) *and* the advantages of a rub (flavoring and a crusty exterior).

Master Class: Making a Basic Marinade

Making a marinade is a lot like constructing a salad dressing—you've got your oil, your vinegar, and your flavorings. But the proportions are different. For this basic marinade, you want to balance the oil against the vinegar, so use equal amounts. Salt and sugar both bring out flavor. For a little more flavor, add the universal seasoning: garlic.

It's not rocket science to put together a marinade, but we are going to follow the rules for making a vinaigrette. You combine the flavorings with the vinegar, then slowly whisk in the oil. This is the best way to get the oil evenly mixed, or emulsified, into the vinegar mixture, since oil is heavier than vinegar. A bowl of marinade with a hunk of meat in it is not like a bottle of salad dressing. You can't shake it up to mix. So it's best to get the oil completely emulsified before you place the meat in it. Do it with a whisk in small quantities, or in a blender, adding the oil slowly.

STEP ONE: MAKE THE BASIC MARINADE.

Basic Marinade

Makes about 1 cup

½ cup white wine vinegar
2 teaspoons sea salt
2 teaspoons sugar
1 teaspoon black pepper
2 garlic cloves, pressed
½ cup olive oil

In a nonreactive bowl, combine the vinegar with the salt, sugar, pepper, and garlic. Blend well with a wire whisk until the salt and sugar are dissolved. Slowly beat in the oil to emulsify the mixture. This is a good basic marinade, but you don't have to stop here.

STEP TWO: ADD ADDITIONAL FLAVOR ELEMENTS.

Choose *one* or *more* of the following to add to the basic marinade mixture:

1. 2 teaspoons dry mustard powder
2. 2 teaspoons anchovy paste (Yes, anchovies are a very good addition!)
3. 1 teaspoon dried oregano
4. 2 teaspoons dried basil

STEP THREE: MARINATE THE MEAT.

Put the meat in a shallow nonreactive bowl (like a glass baking dish) or in a large zippered plastic bag. Pour the marinade over the meat; then turn the meat to coat it evenly. Refrigerate the meat in the marinade.

The table below gives typical marinating times. Exceptions are noted in specific recipes. For example, a marinade with a high acid content might require a briefer marinating time for fish than is listed below. The acid in a marinade can literally cook—or chemically alter—the meat, which is the principle behind dishes like ceviche, in which the fish is cooked by marination, not by heat.

Meat	Marinating Time in Hours
beef steaks	4 to 6
beef kabobs	4 to 6
beef roast, brisket	5 to 7
beef short ribs	6 to 8
pork tenderloins	3 to 4
pork chops	3 to 4
spare ribs	6 to 8
lamb kabobs	4 to 6
venison	6 to 8
chicken breasts	2 to 4
chicken parts	4
chicken wings	6 to 8
split, whole chickens	4
turkey	4 to overnight
turkey quarters	4 to 8
duck	6 to 8
game birds	4 to 6
fish	1 to 2
shellfish	½ to 1

Basic Herbed Marinade

It doesn't get much more basic than this, but, if you're in the mood, you can fiddle around with this recipe on your own or try the suggested variations. If you use this herbed marinade with grilled foods, you'll give them a Mediterranean flavorprint.

Makes about 3/4 cup

3 tablespoons white vinegar
2 tablespoons fresh lemon juice
2 teaspoons salt
1 teaspoon granulated garlic
1 teaspoon granulated onion
1 teaspoon black pepper
1 teaspoon dried basil, crumbled
1 teaspoon dry mustard powder
½ cup olive oil

In a nonreactive bowl, combine the vinegar with the lemon juice, salt, garlic, onion, pepper, basil, and mustard. Blend the mixture well, until the salt is dissolved. With a wire whisk, beat in the oil, a little at a time, until the mixture is emulsified.

Use the marinade immediately, or store it in an airtight jar in the refrigerator for up to 1 month. Allow the mixture to come to room temperature before using.

■ **How to Use It:** This basic marinade is a good choice for chicken, fish, or shellfish since the flavoring is so delicate. Marinate whole chickens for 2 to 4 hours, cut pieces for 2 hours. Because of the marinade's significant acid content, don't marinate fish or shellfish longer than 30 minutes, or the flesh may start to "cook." I prefer to use this recipe with meats for the grill (steaks, tenderloins, chops) that won't take on a heavy smoke flavor, which can overwhelm this marinade. Marinate these meats for 3 to 5 hours.

■ **Variations:** You can substitute any wine vinegar or flavored vinegar for the white vinegar, which tones down the acidity somewhat. Keep an open mind about herbs to replace the basil—dill, oregano, savory, tarragon, rosemary, or thyme are all good choices.

Italian Salad Dressing Marinade

This recipe can do double-duty as a salad dressing or as a marinade. If you're going to use it as a dressing, use extra-virgin olive oil to get the best flavor. In a marinade the subtle fruity flavor of a high-quality (expensive) olive oil is less important.

Makes about 1 3/4 cups

½ cup white wine vinegar
2 tablespoons sugar
1 tablespoon minced garlic
1 tablespoon fresh oregano leaves, minced
1 tablespoon minced fresh parsley
1 teaspoon salt
½ teaspoon white pepper
1 cup olive oil

Combine the vinegar, sugar, garlic, oregano, parsley, salt, and pepper in a nonreactive bowl. Mix well. With a wire whisk, beat in the oil, a little at a time, until the mixture is emulsified.

Use the marinade immediately, or store it in an airtight jar in the refrigerator for up to 1 month. Allow the mixture to come to room temperature before using.

■ **How to Use It:** Use this to marinate larger cuts of beef for 5 to 7 hours, chicken for 2 to 4 hours, or turkey for 4 to 6 hours. It is also good on vegetables—brush some on before grilling.

■ **Variations:** The herb choices aren't set in stone. Basil or rosemary, instead of the oregano, works well if you are marinating chicken. For turkey or beef, try rosemary or thyme.

Spicy Italian Dressing Marinade

This is a large-quantity marinade, good for a whole brisket or turkey. It also makes a decent salad dressing. I'd use extra-virgin olive oil if I were planning to use it as a salad dressing.

Makes about 4 cups

1   cup white vinegar
½   cup white wine vinegar
¼   cup water
¼   cup grated onion
1   tablespoon crushed red pepper
1   tablespoon minced fresh basil
1   tablespoon minced fresh parsley
2   teaspoons minced garlic
1   teaspoon salt
¼   teaspoon white pepper
2   cups vegetable oil

Combine the vinegars, water, onion, red pepper, basil, parsley, garlic, salt, and white pepper in a nonreactive bowl. Mix well. With a wire whisk, beat in the oil, a little at a time, until the mixture is emulsified.

Use the marinade immediately, or store it in an airtight jar in the refrigerator for up to 1 month. Allow the mixture to come to room temperature before using.

■ How to Use It: Marinate beef for 2 to 7 hours, depending on the size of the cut; chicken for 2 to 4 hours; or turkey for 4 to 6 hours.

> Marinades are very similar to salad dressing, but have less oil.

Chef Gary's Italian Marinade

Chef Gary Hild, of Kansas City, teaches classes on cooking healthy food and has a catering business. He is also a marathon runner. Gary uses this marinade on boneless, skinless chicken breasts or on fish fillets.

Makes about 3 cups

2 ounces fresh basil leaves, coarsely chopped
4 garlic cloves, smashed
1 cup fresh lemon juice
1 teaspoon salt
1 teaspoon black pepper
2 cups olive oil

Chop the basil and garlic very fine, and mix them together in a nonreactive bowl with the lemon juice, salt, and pepper. With a wire whisk, beat in the oil slowly, until the mixture is emulsified.

Use the marinade immediately, or store it in an airtight jar in the refrigerator for up to 1 week. Allow the mixture to come to room temperature before using.

■ **How to Use It:** I really like this on shrimp, marinated in the shell and then grilled quickly over a charcoal fire. Prepare fish fillets the same way. You can also use this marinade for chicken (marinate for 2 to 4 hours) or beef steaks (2 to 3 hours).

Herbed Lemon Marinade

This marinade is similar to Chef Gary's Italian Marinade, but it's made with dried herbs so you don't have to make a special trip to the grocery store. Also, it is much more acidic. In Gary's recipe, the ratio of oil to acid is 2 to 1. In this marinade, the ratio is reversed: 1 part oil to 2 parts acid.

Makes about ³/4 cup

- ½ cup fresh lemon juice
- 2 tablespoons paprika
- 1 tablespoon granulated onion
- 2 teaspoons dried basil
- 2 teaspoons dried thyme
- 1 teaspoon dried parsley flakes
- 1 teaspoon salt
- ½ teaspoon black pepper
- ¼ cup vegetable oil

In a nonreactive bowl, combine the lemon juice with the paprika, onion, herbs, salt, and pepper. With a wire whisk, slowly beat in the oil, a little at a time, until the marinade is emulsified.

Use the marinade immediately, or store it in an airtight jar in the refrigerator for up to 1 month. Allow the mixture to come to room temperature before using.

■ **How to Use It:** Marinate fish or shellfish for 30 minutes. The paprika will add a nice rosy color to the fish.

■ **Variations:** You can vary the herb choices, if you like. Try using basil and oregano, rosemary and thyme, or thyme and sage. For a less acidic marinade, increase the oil to ½ cup.

A fryer or broiler is a 2 1/2 pound to 4 1/2 pound chicken that is about seven weeks old. Roasting chickens are usually meaty hens, eight to nine weeks old, weighing 5 to 8 pounds, with enough fat to brown well as they roast.

Shortcut Herbed Marinade

This one's for the lazy among you who can't even be bothered to measure out some herbs, or for those of you who don't have much in the way of a spice shelf. This is a good marinade, especially for chicken, and you'll be credited with hard work when you bring the finished dish to the table.

Makes about 1¼ cups

1   package herb salad dressing mix
1   package garlic salad dressing mix
½ cup white wine vinegar
½ cup vegetable oil
1   teaspoon black pepper

In a nonreactive bowl, combine the dressing mixes, vinegar, oil, and pepper. Blend well until the dressing mixes are thoroughly dissolved.

Use the marinade immediately, or store it in an airtight jar in the refrigerator for up to 1 month. Allow the mixture to come to room temperature before using.

■ **How to Use It:** This is a good marinade for chicken—marinate it 2 to 4 hours.

Onion Marinade

Don't cry, it's a great marinade.

Makes about 1 1/2 cups

- ½ cup white vinegar
- 3 tablespoons grated onion
- 2 tablespoons paprika
- 1 tablespoon onion salt
- 1 tablespoon dry mustard powder
- 1 teaspoon garlic powder
- ½ cup vegetable oil

Combine the vinegar and onion in a nonreactive bowl. Add the paprika, onion salt, mustard powder, and garlic powder. Stir until the spices are completely dissolved. With a wire whisk, beat in the oil until the marinade is emulsified.

Use the marinade immediately, or store it in an airtight jar in the refrigerator for up to 2 weeks. Allow the mixture to come to room temperature before using.

■ **How to Use It:** Beef and pork stand up well to the intense onion flavor of this marinade. Marinate beef brisket for 5 to 7 hours or pork shoulder for 4 to 6 hours.

Herbed Lamb Marinade

A leg of lamb makes a fine barbecue, as do lamb ribs. Lamb is eaten a lot in Greece, where mint is a popular ingredient. You could serve this lamb with mint jelly. The Apple and Mint Relish (page 223) also makes a fine accompaniment to lamb prepared with this marinade.

Makes about 1 cup

½ cup Garlic Vinegar (page 50 or see note below)
1 tablespoon sugar
2 teaspoons dried mint leaves
1 teaspoon salt
1 teaspoon black pepper
½ teaspoon MSG (optional)
¼ cup olive oil
¼ cup vegetable oil

In a nonreactive bowl, combine the vinegar with the sugar, mint, salt, pepper, and MSG, if you are using it, and blend well. With a wire whisk, slowly beat in the oils, a little at a time, until the marinade is emulsified.

Use the marinade immediately, or store it in an airtight jar in the refrigerator for up to 1 month. Allow the mixture to come to room temperature before using.

■ **How to Use It:** Marinate lamb roasts or chops for 2 to 4 hours.

> The dangerous temperature range for the storage of uncooked meat is between 40 and 140°F. Keep cold food cold and hot food hot.

Note: If you do not have Garlic Vinegar on hand, combine 4 to 6 cloves of pressed garlic, or 2 teaspoons of granulated garlic, with ½ teaspoon sea salt in a non-reactive pan. Add 1 cup of white vinegar, and simmer the mixture over medium heat for 20 minutes. Let the vinegar cool, and it is ready to use.

Spicy Lamb Marinade

This marinade will give lamb an unusual flavor twist. Lamb is a tender meat that doesn't require lengthy cooking times. It is best served rare.

Makes about 1 1/4 cups

½ cup red wine vinegar
¼ cup sliced pimiento-stuffed olives
2 teaspoons chili powder
1 teaspoon dried basil
1 teaspoon granulated garlic
½ teaspoon Dijon-style mustard
½ cup olive oil

Combine the vinegar, olives, chili powder, basil, garlic, and mustard in a nonreactive bowl. With a wire whisk, beat in the oil, a little at a time, until the marinade is emulsified.

Use the marinade immediately, or store it in an airtight jar in the refrigerator for up to 1 month. Allow the mixture to come to room temperature before using.

■ **How to Use It:** Marinate lamb roasts or chops for 2 to 4 hours.

Kabob Marinade

If you like to grill skewered meats, this is a good marinade to use. You can use it on vegetables, too. When you are grilling kabobs, it's nice to have squares of onions and bell peppers on the kabobs with the meat—they take on a savory taste from the meat juices. But I don't like to see too many vegetables on the same skewers with the meat because they usually cook faster than the meat and end up overcooked.

Makes about 3/4 cup

¼ cup fresh lemon juice
¼ cup grated onion
1 tablespoon Worcestershire sauce
2 garlic cloves, pressed
1 teaspoon ground ginger
1 teaspoon black pepper
½ teaspoon curry powder
½ teaspoon salt
1 bay leaf
¼ cup vegetable oil

Combine the lemon juice, onion, Worcestershire sauce, garlic, ginger, pepper, curry, salt, and bay leaf in a nonreactive bowl. With a wire whisk, slowly beat in the oil to emulsify the marinade.

Use the marinade immediately, or store it in an airtight jar in the refrigerator for up to 2 weeks. Allow the mixture to come to room temperature before using.

■ **How to Use It:** Marinate pieces of beef, pork, lamb, or chicken for 2 to 4 hours.

Lemony Kabob Marinade

This marinade will stick to the meats you put on the skewers because of the ketchup in it, and will add a nice glaze.

Makes about 1 cup

¼ cup fresh lemon juice
2 tablespoons grated lemon zest (peel)
2 tablespoons ketchup (store-bought or homemade, pages 238–40)
1 garlic clove, pressed
1 teaspoon salt
¼ teaspoon dried marjoram
¼ teaspoon crushed dried rosemary leaves
½ cup vegetable oil

Combine the lemon juice, lemon zest, ketchup, garlic, salt, marjoram, and rosemary in a nonreactive bowl. Whisk in the oil until the mixture is emulsified.

Use the marinade immediately, or store it in an airtight jar in the refrigerator for up to 2 weeks. Allow the mixture to come to room temperature before using.

■ **How to Use It:** Marinate fish for 1 hour or chicken for 3 hours. You may want to use some of the marinade as a finishing sauce. Set some aside before marinating the meat; do not reuse any that has been in contact with uncooked meat.

■ **Variations:** Other herbs work well in this marinade, especially basil and thyme.

Five Mustard Marinade

Just about any food that goes well with mustard will benefit from a long soak in this piquant brew.

Makes about 3 cups

½ cup malt vinegar
½ cup balsamic vinegar
2 teaspoons whole yellow mustard seeds
¼ cup Dijon-style mustard
½ cup Pommery whole-grain mustard
1 teaspoon Chinese dry mustard
1 teaspoon dry mustard powder
1 tablespoon minced fresh chives
1 tablespoon minced fresh tarragon
2 teaspoons cracked black peppercorns
1 teaspoon kosher salt
½ cup olive oil

Combine the malt vinegar, balsamic vinegar, and mustard seeds in a nonreactive saucepan. Bring the mixture to a boil. Remove the pan from the heat, and stir in the Dijon-style and Pommery mustards. Blend thoroughly, stirring until smooth. Stir in the Chinese dry mustard, the mustard powder, chives, tarragon, pepper, and salt. Add the oil in a slow, steady stream, beating with a wire whisk to emulsify the marinade.

Let the marinade cool to room temperature or chill before using. Or, store it in an airtight jar in the refrigerator for up to 1 month. Allow the mixture to come to room temperature before using.

■ **How to Use It:** Marinate thick cuts of beef for at least 3 hours, and thin cuts for at least 1 hour. This marinade is excellent with flank steaks and with tenderloins and other steak cuts. It also works with any pork cut, from ribs to loin roast, which should be marinated for at least 3 hours. Marinate lamb for 2 to 4 hours; the recipe is great with legs, ribs, and chops. Marinate cut pieces of chicken for at least 2 hours, whole and split chickens for about 4 hours. Marinate turkey breasts for 3 to 4 hours, whole birds for 4 to 6 hours.

■ **Variation:** Depending on what you are marinating, you can play around with the herbs, adding to or replacing the tarragon. For example, dill, basil, or oregano goes well with chicken; thyme, savory, oregano, or sage is good with beef; and rosemary or sage goes well with lamb or pork.

Creamy Red Marinade

This will remind you of the orange-colored "French" salad dressing—in fact, you can use it as a salad dressing. It's a good marinade choice for poultry.

Makes about 2 cups

½ cup white vinegar
2 tablespoons fresh lemon juice
2 tablespoons sugar
1 teaspoon dry mustard powder
1 teaspoon garlic powder
1 teaspoon onion salt
1 teaspoon fresh-ground black pepper
½ cup ketchup (store-bought or homemade, pages 238–40)
1 cup vegetable oil

In a nonreactive bowl, combine the vinegar, lemon juice, sugar, mustard, garlic powder, onion salt, and pepper. Blend until the spices are dissolved. Beat in the ketchup with a wire whisk. Slowly beat in the vegetable oil to emulsify the marinade.

Use the marinade immediately, or store it in an airtight jar in the refrigerator for up to 1 month. Allow the mixture to come to room temperature before using.

■ **How to Use It:** Marinate turkey for 4 to 6 hours or chicken for 2 to 4 hours. This marinade also makes a fine finishing sauce. Set some aside before marinating the meat; do not reuse any that has been in contact with uncooked meat.

■ **Variations:** For the heat lovers among you, add some spice with 1 tablespoon chili powder or 1 teaspoon crushed red pepper flakes.

Mixing Marinades

Most marinades contain oil to moisten the meat. Usually the oil is whisked in after the other ingredients are combined. Since water and oil don't normally mix, the whisking action helps incorporate the oil. When the oil is evenly distributed throughout the marinade, the mixture is emulsified. Emulsified liquids are thicker and cling better to the meat. You can do the whisking in a blender or food processor, or by hand, using a wire whisk.

Smoky Tomato Marinade

This is another marinade that will leave a nice light glaze on the meat. The liquid smoke guarantees a smoky flavor, making it a good choice for quickly cooked grilled foods.

Makes about 1 cup

¼ cup unseasoned tomato
  sauce
¼ cup vegetable oil
¼ cup red wine vinegar
2 tablespoons sugar
1 tablespoon Worcestershire
  sauce
1 teaspoon liquid smoke
1 teaspoon dry mustard powder
1 teaspoon salt
1 teaspoon black pepper
3 garlic cloves, pressed

Combine all of the ingredients in a nonreactive bowl. Blend them well, until the mixture is smooth and emulsified.

Use the marinade immediately, or store it in an airtight jar in the refrigerator for up to 2 weeks. Allow the mixture to come to room temperature before using.

■ **How to Use It:** I like this one on beef—any cut, from steaks to roasts. Marinate steaks for 2 to 4 hours or roasts for up to 7 hours.

Ginger Marinade

The sweet-sour flavor of this marinade makes it a perfect candidate for ribs. It will leave a light glaze on the meat, but you might want to use it with Ginger Barbecue Sauce (page 168), too. Dieters take note: there is no oil in this marinade.

Makes about 1 3/4 cups

½ cup water
½ cup ketchup (store-bought or homemade, pages 238–40)
½ cup dark brown sugar
¼ cup white vinegar
1 package Italian salad dressing mix
1 tablespoon grated fresh gingerroot
1 teaspoon salt

Combine all of the ingredients in a nonreactive bowl. Blend them well.

Use the marinade immediately, or store it in an airtight jar in the refrigerator for up to 2 weeks. Allow the mixture to come to room temperature before using.

■ **How to Use It:** Use this marinade for chicken (marinate for 2 to 4 hours) or for ribs (3 to 4 hours).

The average American eats 65 pounds of beef a year, while the average barbecuer eats about 90 pounds of beef – as everybody did fifteen years ago.

Patio Steak Marinade

Patio steaks are usually chuck or arm steaks, but they can be whatever the butcher wants to merchandise. Whatever the cut, these steaks aren't going to be tender without marinating and slow cooking.

Makes about 1 3/4 cups

1   8-ounce can unseasoned tomato sauce
¼   cup red wine vinegar
2   tablespoons brown sugar
1   tablespoon Worcestershire sauce
2   teaspoons granulated onion
1   teaspoon lemon pepper
½   teaspoon seasoned salt
½   teaspoon dried tarragon
¼   cup vegetable oil

Combine the tomato sauce, vinegar, brown sugar, Worcestershire, onion, lemon pepper, seasoned salt, and tarragon in a nonreactive bowl. With a wire whisk, beat in the oil, adding a little at a time, until the marinade is emulsified.

Use the marinade immediately, or store it in an airtight jar in the refrigerator for up to 2 weeks. Allow the mixture to come to room temperature before using.

■ **How to Use It:** Marinate any beef steak with texture (cuts of beef that have a coarser grain to them, such as flank, chuck, or arm steaks) for 2 to 5 hours. Don't use this on a tender prime cut. You may want to use some of the marinade as a finishing sauce. Set some aside before marinating the meat; do not reuse any that has been in contact with uncooked meat.

■ **Variation:** Tarragon isn't the only herb that will work in this marinade. Try something else from the shelf—basil, oregano, savory, celery seed, chili powder, barbecue spice, you name it.

Zesty Patio Steak Marinade

This steak marinade gets a nice zing from the horseradish.

Makes about 2 cups

1   8-ounce can unseasoned tomato sauce
¼   cup vegetable oil
¼   cup A.1. steak sauce
3   tablespoons white vinegar
2   tablespoons prepared horseradish
2   tablespoons brown sugar
1   teaspoon sea salt
1   teaspoon black pepper
½   teaspoon MSG (optional)

Combine the tomato sauce, oil, steak sauce, vinegar, horse-radish, sugar, salt, pepper, and MSG, if you are using it, in a nonreactive saucepan. Simmer over medium heat for 10 minutes, stirring occasionally. Let cool to room temperature before using.

Use the marinade immediately, or store it in an airtight jar in the refrigerator for up to 2 weeks. Allow the mixture to come to room temperature before using.

■ **How to Use It:** Marinate beef steaks 3 to 5 hours. You can also set aside some of the marinade to use as a table sauce. Punch it up with extra horseradish if you like horseradish as much as I do.

Mexican-Style Marinade

Barbecue is one of the grand joys of eating!

If you can't find Mexican brown sugar, which has a strong molasses flavor, substitute regular brown sugar.

Makes about 2 3/4 cups

- 2 cups tomato juice
- ½ cup fresh lime juice
- 2 tablespoons Mexican brown sugar (available in Latino and health food stores)
- 1 tablespoon Heinz 57 Steak Sauce
- 2 teaspoons chili powder
- 1 teaspoon ground cumin
- 1 teaspoon crushed pequín chiles
- 1 teaspoon salt
- ½ teaspoon MSG (optional)
- ¼ teaspoon ground celery seed

Combine all of the ingredients in a nonreactive bowl, and blend well.

Use the marinade immediately, or store it in an airtight jar in the refrigerator for up to 2 weeks. Allow the mixture to come to room temperature before using.

■ **How to Use It:** This is a great marinade for meat to put in tacos. Marinate pork shoulder for 3 to 5 hours or brisket for 4 to 6 hours. Then barbecue it, and chop the meat as you would for a barbecue sandwich. Corn tortillas can replace the white bread buns, and salsa can replace the barbecue sauce. You can also use this recipe for chicken, marinating it for 2 to 4 hours.

Dill Pickle Flank Steak Marinade

Just can't bear to toss out all that good pickle juice? This marinade is a good way to use it—even if it sounds a little weird.

Makes about 2 cups

- ¾ cup dill pickle liquid
- ¼ cup minced dill pickles
- 2 garlic cloves, pressed
- 1 teaspoon black pepper
- ½ teaspoon salt
- 1 cup vegetable oil

Combine the dill pickle liquid, dill pickles, garlic, pepper, and salt in a nonreactive bowl. With a wire whisk, beat in the oil, a little at a time, until the mixture is emulsified.

Use the marinade immediately, or store it in an airtight jar in the refrigerator for up to 2 weeks. Allow the mixture to come to room temperature before using.

■ How to Use It: I like this marinade with flank steak; let it marinate for 3 to 5 hours.

Beefsteak Marinade

Butter and beef stock, rather than oil, provide the liquid base for this marinade. The result is very rich flavor.

Makes about 2 cups

- 1   cup beef stock
- ¼   cup brown sugar
- ¼   cup fresh lemon juice
- 2   tablespoons Worcestershire sauce
- 2   teaspoons garlic salt
- 1   teaspoon black pepper
- 1   bay leaf
- ½   cup (1 stick) unsalted butter

Combine the stock, sugar, lemon juice, Worcestershire sauce, garlic salt, pepper, and bay leaf in a nonreactive saucepan. Simmer for 10 to 15 minutes. Add the butter, and stir to blend it in as it melts. Let the mixture cool to room temperature before using.

Use the marinade immediately, or store it in an airtight jar in the refrigerator for up to 5 days. Allow the mixture to come to room temperature before using.

■ **How to Use It:** Marinate beef brisket or steak for 3 to 7 hours.

Pork Marinade

Why is this marinade especially good with pork? Sometimes it's difficult to identify any one thing in a recipe that makes it work well with another food. It's the combination of all the ingredients. I named this "Pork Marinade" because I found I liked it best with pork.

Makes about 1 1/2 cups

- ½   cup (1 stick) butter
- ½   cup minced onions
- ½   cup Worcestershire sauce
- ¼   cup white vinegar
- 1   teaspoon black pepper

The term "pork barrel" originally referred to a barrel that contained salted pork. A pork barrel was the symbol of wealth and security. It meant that you could feed your family during hard times. The political "pork barrel" symbolizes projects or appropriations that would yield "fat" to benefit a specific locality and/or the constituents of particular legislators.

½ teaspoon salt
½ teaspoon dried thyme
¼ teaspoon dried marjoram

Melt the butter in a nonreactive saucepan over medium heat. Add the onions, and sauté until they are soft. Add the rest of the ingredients, and simmer for 15 minutes, stirring occasionally. Let the marinade cool to room temperature before using.

Use the marinade immediately, or store it in an airtight jar in the refrigerator for up to 5 days. Allow the mixture to come to room temperature before using.

■ **How to Use It:** Marinate pork for 4 to 6 hours; spareribs and short ribs for 3 to 5 hours. Although I recommend it first for

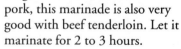

pork, this marinade is also very good with beef tenderloin. Let it marinate for 2 to 3 hours.

■ **Variations:** A little garlic doesn't hurt this marinade's flavor a bit. Add 2 pressed cloves, if you like. You can also substitute red wine vinegar for the white vinegar to mellow the acidity.

Bourbon Pork Marinade

A key ingredient in this marinade is the mustard. Düsseldorf mustard is a German cracked, or grainy, mustard. Other grainy mustards may be substituted, or make up a batch of Coarse Ground Mustard (page 36).

Makes about 2 1/2 cups

½ cup good bourbon, such as Jim Beam
½ cup canola oil
½ cup dark brown sugar, packed
½ cup Düsseldorf mustard
½ cup chicken stock
1 tablespoon rubbed sage
1 teaspoon dried parsley flakes
1 teaspoon salt
1 teaspoon black pepper
½ teaspoon thyme leaves
1 tablespoon butter
1 tablespoon all-purpose flour

Combine the bourbon, oil, brown sugar, mustard, chicken stock, sage, parsley, salt, pepper, and thyme in a nonreactive saucepan. Bring to a boil, stirring constantly. Reduce the heat and simmer for 5 to 6 minutes.

In a small skillet or saucepan, melt the butter. Whisk in the flour to make a roux, or smooth paste. Remove from the heat.

Bring the bourbon mixture to a boil again. Add the roux to the mixture and beat it in with a whisk. Cook until the mixture is thick and smooth. Let it cool to room temperature before using.

Use the marinade immediately, or store it in an airtight jar in the refrigerator for up to 5 days. Allow the mixture to come to room temperature before using.

■ **How to Use It:** Use this on pork, marinating the meat for 3 to 5 hours. It can also be used on beef, which should marinate 3 to 5 hours. If you wish, use some of the marinade as a finishing sauce. Set some aside before marinating the meat; do not reuse any that has been in contact with uncooked meat.

California Pork Marinade

Any dish becomes California-style when it starts getting fruity. This marinade picks up a lot of flavor from the chopped whole orange and lemon. There are quite a few flavors in this one little marinade—and they make a great pork barbecue.

Makes about 2 cups

½ cup cider vinegar
¼ cup chopped unpeeled orange
2 tablespoons chopped unpeeled lemon
½ cup beef stock or water
¼ cup vegetable oil
¼ cup ketchup (store-bought or homemade, pages 238–40)
2 tablespoons Worcestershire sauce
2 tablespoons molasses
1 tablespoon pickling spice, tied in cheesecloth
1 teaspoon dry mustard powder
1 teaspoon black pepper
1 teaspoon cayenne
1 teaspoon salt
1 teaspoon dried mint
½ teaspoon dried basil
½ teaspoon ground allspice
½ teaspoon MSG (optional)

Combine the vinegar, orange, and lemon in a blender or a food processor fitted with a steel blade, and blend until puréed, about 2 minutes. Add the purée to a saucepan, along with the rest of the ingredients. Bring to a boil, reduce the heat, and simmer, uncovered, for 10 to 15 minutes. Allow the marinade to cool to room temperature, and remove and discard the pickling spice in cheesecloth before using.

Use the marinade immediately, or store it in an airtight jar in the refrigerator for up to 1 week. Let the marinade come to room temperature, and remove and discard the pickling spice in cheesecloth, before using.

■ How to Use It: As the title suggests, this is an excellent marinade for pork. Use it to marinate pork shoulders for 5 to 7 hours before cooking.

Orange Chile Marinade

I used this marinade, combined with a rub and finishing sauce, for my pork butt entry at the World Cup in Lisdoonvarna, County Clare, Ireland. Both years I competed there I took first prize. You can't go wrong with this recipe.

Makes about 2 1/2 cups

- 1 cup orange marmalade
- 1 cup ketchup (store-bought or homemade, pages 238–40)
- ½ cup red wine vinegar
- 2 tablespoons chili powder
- 2 tablespoons minced garlic
- 1 tablespoon crushed red pepper
- 2 teaspoons ground cumin
- 1 teaspoon fresh-ground black pepper
- 1 teaspoon sea salt

Combine all of the ingredients in a nonreactive bowl, and blend well.

Use the marinade immediately, or store it in an airtight jar in the refrigerator for up to 1 week. Allow the marinade to come to room temperature before using.

■ **How to Use It:** This is a very versatile marinade. It is excellent for various cuts of pork or beef. Let pork marinate for 4 to 6 hours. Try using it to prepare lamb (let it marinate 3 to 5 hours), poultry (2 to 4 hours), or fish (1 to 2 hours). Set aside some of the marinade beforehand for use as a finishing sauce; do not reuse any that has been in contact with uncooked meat.

Raspberry Marinade

Raspberries are quite an up-and-coming ingredient. You see them in all kinds of foods, from vinaigrettes and salads to poultry and meat dishes. Try this marinade with pork, chicken, or fish.

Makes about 3/4 cup

¼ cup fresh lemon juice
3 tablespoons frozen raspberries, thawed
½ teaspoon dried tarragon
½ teaspoon sea salt
¼ teaspoon white pepper
½ cup vegetable oil

Combine the lemon juice, raspberries, tarragon, salt, and pepper in a nonreactive bowl. Blend well. With a wire whisk, beat in the oil, a little at a time, until the mixture is emulsified.

Use the marinade immediately, or store it in an airtight jar in the refrigerator for up to 1 week. Allow the marinade to come to room temperature before using.

■ **How to Use It:** Use this marinade on pork ribs (marinate 3 to 4 hours), poultry (2 to 4 hours), or fish (1 to 2 hours).

Cornish hens are 5 to 6 weeks old, and weigh about 2 pounds. They are a cross between White Rock and Cornish bloodlines and have a slightly gamy flavor.

Raspberry Margarita Marinade

This recipe goes back to the idea that salad dressing and marinades are close relatives. I had first developed this as a raspberry margarita salad dressing for Adam's Rib Barbecue in Overland Park, Kansas (alas, now closed). The salad dressing was a hit, so when Adam wanted me to come up with some dinner specials, I modified the dressing into this marinade, which he used for grilled shrimp, scallops, and fillet of sole.

Makes about 1 1/4 cups

¼ cup fresh or frozen raspberries
2 garlic cloves, pressed
1 tablespoon sugar
1 teaspoon sea salt
¼ cup fresh lime juice
1½ tablespoons tequila
1½ tablespoons Triple Sec or other orange-flavored liqueur
1 serrano chile, seeded and minced
½ teaspoon ground cumin
½ cup vegetable oil

Combine the raspberries, garlic, sugar, and salt in a nonreactive bowl, and mash to a purée. Add the lime juice, tequila, Triple Sec or other liqueur, serrano pepper, and cumin. Blend well. With a wire whisk, beat in the oil, a little at a time, until the mixture is emulsified.

Use the marinade immediately, or store it in an airtight jar in the refrigerator for up to 1 week. Allow the marinade to come to room temperature before using.

■ **How to Use It:** Use to marinate fish for 1 to 2 hours, or shrimp for ½ to 1 hour.

Caribbean Citrus Marinade

When I think of Caribbean food, I think of very hot chile peppers. Well, food that has Caribbean flavors isn't always super hot. This marinade is a good example. It has a little heat, and a lot of flavor.

Makes about 1 1/2 cups

¼ cup grapefruit juice
¼ cup chicken stock
¼ cup red wine vinegar
2 tablespoons sugar
1 tablespoon Jerk Seasoning (page 25)
1 tablespoon orange zest (peel)
3 garlic cloves, pressed
1 teaspoon sea salt
1 teaspoon black pepper
½ cup vegetable oil

Combine the grapefruit juice, stock, vinegar, sugar, Jerk Seasoning, orange zest, garlic, salt, and pepper in a nonreactive bowl. Blend well. With a wire whisk, beat in the oil, a little at a time, until the mixture is emulsified.

Use the marinade immediately, or store it in an airtight jar in the refrigerator for 4 to 5 days. Allow the marinade to come to room temperature before using.

■ **How to Use It:** Marinate beef brisket for 5 to 7 hours or pork shoulder for 5 to 7 hours. Try it on chicken (marinate for 2 to 4 hours) or fish (1 to 2 hours).

Orange Blossom Marinade

This recipe is called Orange Blossom Marinade because I took its central flavors from a cocktail of the same name, made of orange juice, champagne, and honey. My marinade uses the orange juice and the honey, with champagne vinegar for a hint of champagne flavor. The mustard and other ingredients round it out.

Makes about 2 cups

½ cup orange juice concentrate
½ cup champagne vinegar
½ cup clover honey
¼ cup prepared yellow mustard
2 tablespoons soy sauce
1 teaspoon granulated onion
2 garlic cloves, pressed
1 teaspoon ground ginger
1 teaspoon salt

Combine all of the ingredients in a nonreactive saucepan. Simmer over medium heat for 10 to 15 minutes, stirring occasionally. Let it cool to room temperature before using.

Use the marinade immediately, or store it in an airtight jar in the refrigerator for up to 2 weeks. Allow the marinade to come to room temperature before using.

■ **How to Use It:** Marinate chicken for 3 to 5 hours, or fish for 1 to 2 hours.

Honey-Mint Marinade

This is a very light and delicate, but tasty, marinade I think you will enjoy.

Makes about 1 1/2 cups

1 cup apple cider or juice
⅓ cup clover honey
2 tablespoons white wine vinegar
2 tablespoons canola oil

2   teaspoons dried mint leaves
1   teaspoon salt
½   teaspoon white pepper

Combine all of the ingredients, and blend well.

Use the marinade immediately, or store it in an airtight jar in the refrigerator for up to 1 month. Allow the mixture to come to room temperature before using.

■ **How to Use It:** Marinate chicken for 2 to 4 hours, or fish for 1 to 2 hours.

Apple Jelly Marinade

I have used apple jelly and cinnamon apple jelly in several glazes, and like them very well. So this marinade is the next step in the progression.

Makes about 2 ¼ cups

¼   cup apple jelly
¼   cup chicken stock
¼   cup white or cider vinegar
2   tablespoons fresh lemon juice
1   tablespoon prepared yellow mustard
1   tablespoon soy sauce
1   teaspoon minced fresh parsley
1   teaspoon crushed dried rosemary
1   teaspoon salt
½   teaspoon black pepper
½   teaspoon celery seeds
½   teaspoon MSG (optional)
¼   cup vegetable oil

Combine the jelly and chicken stock in a nonreactive saucepan over low heat. Stir until the jelly is melted into the stock. Add the vinegar, lemon juice, mustard, soy sauce, parsley, rosemary, salt, pepper, celery seeds, and MSG, if you are using it. Simmer the mixture for 10 minutes, stirring occasionally. Blend in the oil with a wire whisk. Let the mixture cool to room temperature before using.

Use the marinade immediately, or store it in an airtight jar in the refrigerator for up to 1 week. Allow the mixture to come to room temperature before using.

■ **How to Use It:** Marinate pork ribs for 3 to 4 hours, or fish for 1 to 2 hours.

Parsley Ginger Marinade

Although I don't use it all that much, soda pop is a pretty common ingredient in marinades. In this one, ginger ale teams up with fresh ginger root to provide the dominant flavor.

Makes about 1 3/4 cups

½ cup vegetable oil
⅓ cup wine vinegar
⅓ cup ginger ale
¼ cup minced fresh parsley
¼ cup minced green onions, green and white parts
2 tablespoons grated fresh gingerroot
2 tablespoons sugar
1 teaspoon salt
2 garlic cloves, pressed

Combine all of the ingredients in a nonreactive bowl, and blend well.

Use the marinade immediately, or store it in an airtight jar in the refrigerator for up to 2 weeks. The ginger flavor will become more pronounced the longer it is stored. Allow the mixture to come to room temperature before using.

■ **How to Use It:** Marinate chicken for 2 to 4 hours, or fish for 1 to 2 hours.

Pineapple Marinade

Compared to the Hawaiian Marinade that follows, this marinade is rather sweet.

Makes about 2 cups

1   cup pineapple juice
¾   cup dark brown sugar
1   tablespoon white vinegar
1   tablespoon prepared yellow mustard
1   tablespoon soy sauce
1   teaspoon dry mustard powder
1   teaspoon salt

Combine all of the ingredients in a nonreactive bowl, and blend well.

Use the marinade immediately, or store it in an airtight jar in the refrigerator for up to 1 month. Allow the mixture to come to room temperature before using.

■ **How to Use It:** Marinate country-style ribs for 3 to 4 hours, or chicken for 2 to 4 hours.

Hawaiian Marinade

This recipe signals a shift in my recipes toward the Pacific Rim, or, as I call it, the "Oriental Phenomenon." This marinade is garlicky, gingery, salty, and sweet-and-sour, all at once.

Makes about 2 3/4 cups

1   cup pineapple juice
½   cup soy sauce
½   cup Garlic Vinegar (page 50 or see Note below)
2   tablespoons grated fresh gingerroot
2   garlic cloves, pressed
1   teaspoon black pepper
½   cup sesame oil
¼   cup canola oil

Combine the pineapple juice, soy sauce, vinegar, ginger, garlic, and pepper in a nonreactive mixing bowl. In a separate bowl, mix the two oils. Using a wire whisk, beat the combined oils into the pineapple mixture, a little at a time, until the mixture is emulsified.

Use the marinade immediately, or store it in an airtight jar in the refrigerator for up to 1 week. Allow the mixture to come to room temperature before using.

■ **How to Use It:** Use this marinade for pork chops or ribs, or for chicken—each should be marinated 2 to 4 hours.

Note: If you do not have Garlic Vinegar on hand, combine 4 to 6 cloves of pressed garlic, or 2 teaspoons of granulated garlic, with ½ teaspoon sea salt in a nonreactive pan. Add 1 cup of white vinegar, and simmer the mixture over medium heat for 20 minutes. Let the vinegar cool, and it is ready to use.

Korean Beef Marinade

What is called Korean barbecue is really grilling over charcoal.
In restaurants, it is often done right at the table. Before grilling,
the meat is usually marinated in a delicious garlic and soy
sauce–based marinade such as this one.

Makes about 3 cups

- 1 cup soy sauce or light-colored soy sauce
- 1 cup sugar
- ½ cup toasted sesame seeds*
- 2 tablespoons white wine vinegar
- 4 garlic cloves, smashed
- 1 tablespoon grated fresh gingerroot
- 1 teaspoon black pepper
- 1 teaspoon salt
- 1 cup vegetable oil

Combine the soy sauce, sugar, sesame seeds, vinegar, garlic,
ginger, pepper, and salt in a food processor fitted with a steel
blade. Process until the garlic is minced and the spices dissolved,
about 2 to 3 minutes. Add the oil slowly in a steady stream, and
process until the mixture is emulsified.

Use the marinade immediately, or store it in an airtight jar
in the refrigerator for up to 1 week. Allow the mixture to come
to room temperature before using.

> I would choose a charcoal
> grill over a gas or electric
> grill anytime, but if I did
> have a gas or electric grill,
> I would find out how to
> use it to cook the best
> barbecue possible.

■ **How to Use It:** Marinate
beef short ribs or flank steak
for 3 to 5 hours.

*Note: To toast the sesame
seeds, place them in a dry
skillet over medium heat and
toast, stirring frequently, until
they are golden and fragrant,
about 4 minutes. Take care
that the seeds do not scorch,
or they will taste bitter.

Teriyaki Marinade and Sauce

You can buy bottled teriyaki sauce, but why bother? This version is simple, with an uncomplicated flavor. This teriyaki recipe is higher in acidity than those that follow.

Makes about 1 1/4 cups

½ cup soy sauce
½ cup fresh lemon juice
¼ cup vegetable oil
1 garlic clove, pressed
½ teaspoon ground ginger

Combine all of the ingredients in a nonreactive bowl, and blend well.

Use the marinade immediately, or store it for up to 1 week in an airtight jar in the refrigerator. Allow the mixture to come to room temperature before using.

■ **How to Use It:** You can use this as a marinade or as a dipping sauce, but once meat has soaked in it, do not reuse it. Make up a fresh batch of the marinade just for dipping.

Let beef steak marinate for 2 to 4 hours. Or use it on pork shoulder or pork butt (marinate 3 to 5 hours), chicken (2 to 4 hours), or seafood such as tuna, shark, or swordfish (1 to 2 hours).

■ **Variation:** To create a marinade with lower acidity, replace ¼ cup of the lemon juice with orange juice. For a more complexly flavored marinade, use 2 tablespoons sesame oil and 2 tablespoons canola or peanut oil in place of the ¼ cup vegetable oil.

> Always use the best products and ingredients available to you—the best charcoal, the best lighter, the best meat—for the best results. One bad link in this chain can ruin the entire experience.

Teriyaki Marinade
for Flank Steak

This Teriyaki Marinade is suited for just about any meat or vegetable. I happen to use it more often for flank steak than I do for fish or vegetables.

Makes about 2 cups

1   cup pineapple juice
½   cup soy sauce
½   cup brown sugar, packed
1   teaspoon grated fresh gingerroot
2   garlic cloves, pressed

Combine all of the ingredients in a nonreactive bowl, and blend well.

Use the marinade immediately, or store it for up to 1 week in the refrigerator. Allow the mixture to come to room temperature before using.

■ **How to Use It:** You can use this as a marinade or as a dipping sauce, but once meat has soaked in it, do not reuse it. Make up a fresh batch of the marinade just for dipping.

This marinade is especially good for flank steaks, or use it for sirloin or rib-eye steaks. Marinate the steaks 2 to 4 hours.

■ **Variation:** You can increase the ginger to 1 tablespoon if you like a stronger ginger flavor.

Rosy Teriyaki Marinade and Dipping Sauce

The flavors in this recipe are more complex than in the preceding teriyaki marinades. This marinade leaves a nice glaze on grilled meats.

Makes about 1 1/2 cups

½ cup pineapple juice
⅓ cup molasses
¼ cup soy sauce
¼ cup ketchup (store-bought or homemade, pages 238–40)
¼ cup grated onion
1 teaspoon ground ginger

Combine all of the ingredients in a nonreactive bowl, and blend well.

Use the marinade immediately, or store it for up to 2 weeks in the refrigerator. Allow the mixture to come to room temperature before using.

■ **How to Use It:** You can use this as a marinade or as a dipping sauce, but once meat has soaked in it, do not reuse it. Make up a fresh batch of the marinade just for dipping.

Use this to marinate beef steaks, pork ribs, or chicken, for 2 to 4 hours, or fish for 1 to 2 hours.

■ **Variation:** Replace the onion with 2 cloves of garlic, minced. Add 4 finely chopped scallions, too.

Low-Sodium Soy Sauce

If you need to cut down on sodium in your diet, you can use a low-sodium soy sauce in any of these marinades, without any loss in flavor.

Pineapple-Sesame Marinade

Light, sweet, and versatile, this is a good marinade for grilled
stir-fry of any kind.

Makes about 1 3/4 cups

1   cup pineapple juice
¼   cup soy sauce
2   tablespoons clover honey
2   teaspoons minced fresh gingerroot
2   teaspoons toasted sesame seeds*
¼   cup vegetable oil
2   tablespoons sesame oil

Combine the pineapple juice, soy sauce, honey, ginger, and
sesame seeds in a nonreactive bowl. In a separate bowl, mix the
two oils. Using a wire whisk, slowly beat in the combined oils, a
little at a time, until the mixture is emulsified.

Use the marinade immediately, or store it in the refrigerator
for up to 2 weeks. Allow the mixture to come to room
temperature before using.

■ **How to Use It:** Marinate beef chuck roast for 5 to 7 hours,
pork butt or ribs for 3 to 5 hours, chicken for 2 to 4 hours, or
fish for 1 to 2 hours.

*Note: To toast the sesame seeds, place them in a dry skillet
over medium heat and toast, stirring frequently, until they are
golden and fragrant, about 4 minutes. Take care that the seeds
do not scorch, or they will taste bitter.

Polynesian Marinade

Spicy, sweet, and salty, this marinade leaves a nice glaze on
grilled meats.

Makes about 1³/4 cups

1   cup soy sauce
½   cup clover honey
¼   cup sweet sherry
2   tablespoons minced candied ginger
3   garlic cloves, minced
1   teaspoon curry powder
1   teaspoon sea salt
½   teaspoon ground cinnamon
½   teaspoon ground cloves

Combine all of the ingredients in a nonreactive bowl, and blend
well.

Use the marinade immediately, or store it in the refrigerator
for up to 2 weeks. Allow the mixture to come to room
temperature before using.

■ How to Use It: Marinate beef steak for 2 to 4 hours, pork ribs
or butt for 3 to 5 hours, or chicken for 2 to 4 hours.

Ginger Orange Marinade

This is a good marinade for the health conscious.

Makes about 1 1/2 cups

½   cup orange juice
½   cup light (low-sodium) soy sauce
2   tablespoons grated fresh gingerroot
1   tablespoon grated or minced lemon zest (peel)
3   garlic cloves, pressed
½   cup canola oil

Combine the orange juice, soy sauce, ginger, lemon zest, and
garlic in a nonreactive bowl, and blend well. With a wire whisk,
beat in the oil, a little at a time, until the mixture is emulsified.

Use the marinade immediately, or store it in the refrigerator for up to 1 week. Allow it to come to room temperature before using.

■ **How to Use It:** This marinade is an excellent one for chicken. Marinate it 2 to 4 hours.

■ **Variation:** This is a healthy recipe, calling for canola oil and light soy sauce. But there is no reason you can't use regular soy sauce instead, and replace the canola oil with another oil. You could, for example, use ¼ cup sesame oil and ¼ cup peanut oil to give the marinade a strong Chinese flavorprint.

Char Siu Chinese Marinade

Char siu pork is the unnaturally red-colored meat you see hanging in the window of Chinese food shops. This marinade will give you the same great taste, and color, too, if you use the food coloring. You can find the hoisin sauce and five-spice seasoning in Chinese grocery stores, specialty food stores, and many supermarkets.

Makes about 1 ¼ cups

½ cup sugar
3 tablespoons sweet sherry
2 tablespoons soy sauce
½ cup hoisin sauce
2 teaspoons minced fresh gingerroot
½ teaspoon five-spice powder
1 teaspoon salt
½ teaspoon red food coloring (optional)

In a nonreactive bowl, dissolve the sugar in the sherry and soy sauce. Add the hoisin sauce, ginger, five-spice seasoning, salt, and red food coloring if you are using it, and blend well.

Use the marinade immediately, or store it in the refrigerator for up to 2 weeks. Allow the mixture to come to room temperature before using.

■ **How to Use It:** This is meant to be used with pork, but it goes quite well with chicken and duck, too. I'd skip the food coloring with poultry, though. Marinate pork strips and ribs for 2 to 4 hours, chicken for 2 to 3 hours, or duck for 2 to 5 hours.

■ **Variation:** This can be used as a glaze for grilled meats. Reduce the amount of sugar to 2 tablespoons.

Chinese Barbecue Marinade

There's a lot of sugar in this marinade, and it clings well to the meat. So be sure to cook over indirect heat to prevent the meat from charring.

Makes about 1 1/2 cups

- ½ cup soy sauce
- ½ cup hoisin sauce
- ½ cup clover honey
- 2 tablespoons sweet sherry
- 2 teaspoons grated fresh gingerroot
- 1 teaspoon salt
- 1 teaspoon red food coloring (optional)

Combine all of the ingredients in a nonreactive bowl, and blend well.

Use the marinade immediately, or store it in the refrigerator for up to 2 weeks. Allow the mixture to come to room temperature before using.

■ **How to Use It:** Marinate pork shoulder for 3 to 5 hours, chicken for 2 to 4 hours, or duck for 2 to 5 hours. You can also use this marinade as a finishing sauce. Set some aside before marinating the meat; do not reuse any that has been in contact with uncooked meat. For a finishing sauce, paint it on the meat about halfway through the cooking process.

■ **Variation:** This can be used as a glaze for grilled meat. Reduce the amount of honey to 1 tablespoon.

> The oldest known barbecue pit is in the small village of Banpo, near Xian in East-Central China, and dates back to 6,000 B.C.

■ ■ ■

A Chinese Flavorprint

Five-spice powder is a Chinese flavorprint spice blend.
One taste—or one sniff—and you know you aren't in
Kansas anymore. The five spices in this ancient blend are
Sichuan peppercorns, cassia or cinnamon bark, star anise,
cloves, and fennel seed.

■ ■ ■

Chinese Beef Marinade

This is one of my favorite marinades. In addition to using it on
steaks, I marinate pieces of beef (sirloin steak sliced thin) and
stir-fry them with peapods in my grill wok.

Makes about 1 1/4 cups

½ cup soy sauce
½ cup brown sugar, packed
¼ cup sherry
1 tablespoon sugar
1 tablespoon ground cinnamon
2 teaspoons ground anise
1 teaspoon ground cloves

Combine all of the ingredients in a nonreactive bowl, and blend
well.

Use the marinade immediately, or store it in the refrigerator
for up to 2 weeks. Allow the mixture to come to room
temperature before using.

■ **How to Use It:** Marinate beef steaks for 2 to 4 hours.

Spicy Fish Marinade

Here's another marinade with a less conventional flavor combination—this one hails from Southeast Asia.

Makes about 1 cup

- ¼ cup soy sauce
- ¼ cup fresh lime juice
- ¼ cup thinly sliced onion
- 1 tablespoon brown sugar
- 2 teaspoons ground coriander
- 1 teaspoon cumin
- 1 teaspoon salt
- 1 teaspoon black pepper
- 1 teaspoon crushed red pepper
- ½ teaspoon ground ginger
- ¼ teaspoon MSG (optional)
- ¼ cup peanut or olive oil

In a nonreactive bowl, combine the soy sauce, lime juice, onion, brown sugar, coriander, cumin, salt, black pepper, red pepper, ginger, and MSG, if you are using it. With a wire whisk, beat in the oil, a little at a time, until the mixture is emulsified.

Use the marinade immediately, or store it in the refrigerator for up to 1 week. Allow the mixture to come to room temperature before using.

■ **How to Use It:** Marinate fish or shrimp for 1 to 2 hours. This marinade may also be used on chicken. Marinate it 2 to 4 hours.

Spicy Tandoori Marinade

They've been barbecuing chicken in India since ancient times in barrel-shaped mud or clay ovens called tandoors. The ovens are charcoal-fired, and they generate a fierce heat that quickly seals the outside of the bird, leaving it moist and tender on the inside. This yogurt-based marinade is a typical treatment for the chicken before it goes into the tandoor. The marinade will cling to the chicken and form a nice crust.

Makes about 1 3/4 cups

⅛ teaspoon saffron threads
2 tablespoons boiling water
1½ cups plain yogurt
¼ cup fresh lemon juice
2 tablespoons paprika
2 teaspoons grated fresh gingerroot
2 garlic cloves, pressed
1 jalapeño, seeded and minced
2 teaspoons ground coriander
1 teaspoon curry powder
1 teaspoon ground cumin
1 teaspoon cayenne
1 teaspoon salt

In a nonreactive bowl, dissolve the saffron in the boiling water. Stir in the yogurt, lemon juice, paprika, ginger, garlic, jalapeño, coriander, curry, cumin, cayenne, and salt. Blend well. Use immediately.

■ **How to Use It:** Marinate pieces of chicken for kabobs for 1 to 2 hours, or chicken parts for 2 to 4 hours. I like to use this marinade for turkey legs. Turkey parts should be marinated for 4 to 6 hours. If you are making kabobs, set aside some of the marinade beforehand to brush on the vegetables before grilling.

Tandoori Marinade

There are many variations of tandoori marinades. This one has less heat than the previous one, but more aromatic spices. Tandoori marinades are good for kabobs; the marinade forms a nice crust on the meat and vegetables.

Makes about 1½ cups

1   cup plain yogurt
¼   cup peanut oil
1   small onion, minced
2   tablespoons paprika
2   tablespoons fresh lemon juice
1   tablespoon grated fresh gingerroot
2   teaspoons curry powder
4   garlic cloves, pressed
1   teaspoon ground coriander
1   teaspoon ground cardamom
1   teaspoon salt
½   teaspoon ground cumin

Combine all of the ingredients in a nonreactive bowl, and blend until smooth. Use immediately.

■ How to Use It: Marinate pieces of chicken for kabobs for 1 to 2 hours, or chicken parts for 2 to 4 hours. Fish can be marinated for about 1 hour in this marinade. If you are making kabobs, and you wish to brush some of the marinade onto the vegetables before grilling, set some aside before marinating the meat in it.

Buttermilk Marinade

This is a good low-acid marinade for freshwater fish and for game.

Makes about 2 cups

2   cups buttermilk
1   teaspoon fresh rosemary, minced
½   teaspoon dried marjoram

¼ teaspoon ground oregano
2 tablespoons fresh lemon juice

Combine the buttermilk and herbs in a nonreactive bowl, and blend well. Stir in the lemon juice slowly, so as not to curdle the milk. Use immediately.

■ **How to Use It:** Use this marinade for beef eye of round (marinate for 4 to 6 hours), game (2 to 5 hours), or fish (1 to 2 hours). If the flavor of your game is too strong for your taste, you may want to soak it overnight in this marinade.

Minted Turkish Marinade

This marinade is similar in style to a tandoori marinade; yogurt forms the base. The spices called for make a somewhat sweet combination, but the strong flavor of a half cup of fresh mint leaves adds balance.

Makes about 1 1/2 cups

1 cup plain yogurt
½ cup fresh mint leaves, minced
2 tablespoons fresh lemon juice
1 tablespoon grated lemon zest (peel)
3 garlic cloves, pressed
1 teaspoon sea salt
½ teaspoon ground allspice
½ teaspoon ground cinnamon
¼ teaspoon cayenne

Combine all of the ingredients in a nonreactive bowl, and blend with a wire whisk until smooth. Use immediately.

■ **How to Use It:** This is a good marinade for chicken and lamb. Marinate chicken or a leg of lamb for 2 to 4 hours. It is also excellent on fish (marinate for 1 to 2 hours). It's not bad as a dip, either, or serve it as a sauce for grilled chicken or lamb stuffed into pita pockets. Be sure to make up a fresh batch for these uses, though. Don't reuse this marinade once it has been in contact with uncooked meat.

4
Mops, Sops, and Bastes

Mops, sops, and bastes are thin liquids that usually contain an acid and spices, and sometimes oil. They are applied to your barbecue while it is being cooked, to help it retain moisture. They can be simple in flavor—such as apple juice or plain beer—or they can be complex.

The words *mop, sop,* and *baste* are all interchangeable, and what you call them probably depends on where you grew up. The word *mop* came to be used when someone was barbecuing and needed a way to baste the meat. He grabbed one of his wife's clean dish mops to do the job, and thus the name mop.

Most sops and bastes are cooked to blend their flavors. They should be kept warm if they are to be used right away, or reheated if they have been refrigerated—they are always applied warm. Start basting your barbecue after it has cooked for half of its projected cooking time. You want to give the rub a chance to form a crust on the meat before you start applying a baste. The baste will take on a different flavor and character every time you mop with it, because it will pick up flavors from the meat you are basting. Sop, mop, or baste small items every 30 minutes and big items, like brisket, every 45 to 60 minutes. Bring the baste to a simmer each time you apply it, so that you aren't applying a cold liquid to the meat.

> Add extra flavor when grilling fish, chicken breasts, vegetables, or fruit, by placing sprigs of fresh or dried herbs, soaked in water beforehand, over your hot coals.

Mops can be made for mopping only, or they can double as marinades or as finishing sauces. The Brisket Marinade and Mop (page 144) is a good example of a recipe that doubles as a mop and a marinade. If you plan to use a recipe as both mop and marinade, divide the batch into two parts, using one portion to

marinate the meat and the other to baste it. In between the marinade and the mop, you should also apply a rub to give the meat a nice crust.

Another word of advice: If you are making a larger quantity of mop than you think you will use in one day, it is a good idea to pour some off and hold it in reserve. That way the mop or brush, which keeps touching the uncooked meat, doesn't contaminate the remaining baste with bacteria. Another option is to use the baste just half a cup at a time, and add to it from your reserve as you need it.

You don't need a master class to teach you how to construct a mop, but if you look at the first recipe in this chapter, Basic Mop or Baste, you will see the essential recipe for a mop.

Basic Mop or Baste

This is a simple mop or baste, and can be changed or expanded upon as you wish. A few suggestions to start with—try sage, mustard, or pepper. Or add any other ingredient you think will enhance the flavor of the meat you are cooking. This recipe makes a larger quantity of marinade than others, and it can be easily doubled or tripled for a crowd.

Makes about 3 cups

1 cup water or stock
1 cup vinegar
1 to 3 teaspoons salt
1 to 2 tablespoons spices
1 cup oil

Combine the water or stock, vinegar, salt, and spices in a nonreactive saucepan. Heat over medium heat, stirring occasionally, until the salt is dissolved and the spices have infused the liquid with their flavor, about 15 minutes. Add the oil and simmer, stirring occasionally, for 15 minutes. Keep the mixture warm. Use it to baste your barbecue after the spices in the rub have set (cooked on, forming a crust on the meat).

Use the baste immediately, or store it in an airtight jar in the refrigerator for up to 1 month. Reheat the baste before using it; apply it warm.

All-Purpose Basting Sauce with Herbs

You add the herbs to this one. Which ones? It's up to you. How much? How much do you think? Okay, try adding up to 2 tablespoons of herbs. And if you are really desperate for advice, use a tried-and-true flavor combination, like herbes de Provence, or a few of the herbs used in it: marjoram, thyme, summer savory, basil, rosemary, sage, and lavender. Be careful not to overpower your baste by using too many different flavors. Also, keep in mind that dry herbs are 2 to 3 times as potent as fresh. You are heating them, too, which brings out their flavoring oils. So add them with a bit of caution.

Makes about 1 3/4 cups

½ cup white wine vinegar
½ cup fresh lemon juice
½ cup vegetable oil
¼ cup soy sauce
1 garlic clove, pressed
½ teaspoon salt
½ teaspoon black pepper
½ teaspoon MSG (optional)
Herbs, fresh or dried

Place all of the ingredients in a nonreactive saucepan and heat, stirring occasionally, for 15 minutes. Keep the baste warm during use.

Use this sauce immediately, or store it in an airtight jar in the refrigerator for up to 2 weeks. Reheat it before using.

■ **How to Use It:** I don't call this "all-purpose" for no reason. Baste with it, mop it on, or brush it on meat, fish, or poultry frequently while barbecuing. If you are cooking a large piece of meat with a rub on it, don't start basting until about halfway through the cooking process.

Smoky All-Purpose Basting Sauce

What the smoke from your fire doesn't have time to add during cooking—say you are grilling fast-cooking meats, like fish steaks or chicken breast fillets—liquid smoke can add instead. Liquid smoke? Gasp! Is that authentic? Well, you know how they make it? They capture smoke in a liquid base. It really *is* liquid smoke.

Makes about 2 cups

- 1 cup water
- 4 beef bouillon cubes
- ¼ cup dark brown sugar
- ¼ cup pure maple syrup
- 2 tablespoons soy sauce
- 2 tablespoons Worcestershire sauce
- 1 tablespoon seasoned salt
- 1 tablespoon liquid smoke
- 1 tablespoon Kitchen Bouquet, a caramel coloring (optional)

Place all the ingredients in a nonreactive saucepan and simmer for 20 minutes, stirring occasionally. Remove the pan from heat, and let sit until the sauce has cooled slightly, but is still warm.

Use this sauce immediately, or store it in an airtight jar in the refrigerator for up to 1 week. Reheat it before using.

■ **How to Use It:** When you are grilling fish, chicken pieces or fillets, steaks, hamburgers, or other quick-cooking meats, baste frequently with this sauce.

Mop for All
Barbecue Meats

I like to make my own stock for this, using fresh bones from the butcher shop (see box below). This is a good baste for any kind of barbecue.

Makes about 5 cups

1   quart beef, chicken, or pork stock, homemade or canned
1   cup Worcestershire sauce
¼   cup cider vinegar
¼   cup vegetable oil
2   tablespoons chili powder
2   tablespoons paprika
2   tablespoons seasoned salt
1   tablespoon dry mustard powder
1   tablespoon garlic powder
1   teaspoon cayenne

To make your own stock, preheat the oven to 375°F. Place about 6 pounds of beef, chicken, or pork bones in a roasting pan in a single layer. Bake them in the oven for about 1 hour, or until they are well browned. Remove the bones from the roasting pan and place them in a large stockpot. Add about a quart of water to the roasting pan and loosen as much of the drippings and crumbs as you can. Pour this water into the stockpot, along with 3 more quarts of water. Add 1 chopped carrot; 1 medium-size onion, quartered but not peeled; 3 chopped celery ribs; 2 large unpeeled garlic cloves, smashed; 1 teaspoon whole peppercorns; 1 bay leaf; and 2 tablespoons tomato paste. Bring to a boil, reduce the heat, and simmer for 2 hours. Strain the liquid. You should have about 2 quarts of stock.

½ teaspoon powdered bay leaf
¼ teaspoon MSG (optional)

Combine all the ingredients in a large nonreactive saucepan.
Bring the mixture to a boil, then reduce the heat and simmer,
stirring occasionally, for 15 minutes. Use the mop warm.

Use the mop immediately, or store it in an airtight jar in the
refrigerator for up to 5 days. Reheat it before using.

■ **How to Use It:** Baste this on all types of meat or on poultry.
Sop, mop, or baste small items every 30 minutes and large
items, such as brisket, every 45 to 60 minutes, beginning about
halfway through cooking. Keep the baste simmering so you
don't apply a cold liquid to the meat.

Beef Mop Sauce

This mop has a well-rounded flavor from the beef bouillon base
and the ketchup. Onion, Worcestershire sauce, garlic,
horseradish, and mustard provide the punch.

Makes about 3 cups

2 beef bouillon cubes
2 cups water
½ cup vegetable oil
¼ cup ketchup (store-bought or homemade, pages 238–40)
¼ cup cider vinegar
¼ cup grated onion
2 tablespoons Worcestershire sauce
1 tablespoon sugar
2 garlic cloves, pressed
2 teaspoons grated fresh horseradish
1 teaspoon dry mustard powder
1 teaspoon salt
1 teaspoon black pepper

In a medium-size nonreactive saucepan, heat the bouillon cubes
in the water until they are dissolved. Add the remaining
ingredients and bring the mixture to a boil. Reduce the heat, and
simmer for 30 minutes, stirring occasionally. Use the mop warm.
This mop is best used the same day it is made.

■ **How to Use It:** Mop it on beef. It's a good choice for a brisket, but it'll work on everything from hamburgers to steaks. Sop, mop, or baste on small items every 30 minutes, and on big items, such as brisket, every 45 to 60 minutes, beginning about halfway through cooking. Keep the baste simmering so you aren't applying a cold liquid to the meat.

Brisket Marinade and Mop

Match this marinade and mop with a rub from chapter 2, and you will have a championship barbecue. Rubs that would be good choices include the Sample Master Class Barbecue Rub (page 62) and Bill's Beef Power Rub (page 67).

Makes about 4 cups

2   cups beef stock
1   cup ketchup (store-bought or homemade, pages 238–40)
½ cup fresh lemon juice
½ cup Worcestershire sauce
2   tablespoons liquid smoke
1   tablespoon chili powder
2   teaspoons celery seeds
2   teaspoons seasoned salt
1   teaspoon granulated onion

Combine all of the ingredients in a nonreactive saucepan and simmer for 15 minutes, stirring occasionally. Remove the pan from heat, and let sit until the sauce has cooled slightly, but is still warm. Use immediately.

■ **How to Use It:** Pour over a 7- to 9-pound brisket, and marinate for 4 to 6 hours. Remove the brisket, pat it dry with paper towels, and season with your rub. Begin cooking as desired. For a mop: Make a second batch of the recipe, reducing all of the quantities by one half. Keep the liquid warm and baste with it frequently, beginning about halfway through cooking.

The Ultimate Beef Baste

Is this the ultimate baste? Well, it's a rich one, with butter and mushrooms. It makes a high-class barbecue.

Makes about 3 cups

¼ cup (½ stick) butter
5 garlic cloves, pressed
½ pound white button mushrooms, sliced
1 cup ketchup (store-bought or homemade, pages 238–40)
2 cups rich beef stock*
½ cup Worcestershire sauce
1 teaspoon black pepper
1 teaspoon sea salt

Melt the butter in a nonreactive saucepan over medium-high heat. Add the garlic and sauté, stirring constantly, for 1 minute. Add the mushrooms and sauté until they are golden, about 3 minutes. Blend in the ketchup, stock, Worcestershire sauce, pepper, and salt. Bring the mixture to a boil. Reduce the heat and simmer for 30 to 45 minutes. Use the baste warm.

Use this baste immediately; do not store it in the refrigerator.

■ **How to Use It:** This is good on brisket, ribs, and steaks. Sop, mop, or baste on small items every 30 minutes, and on big items, such as brisket, every 45 to 60 minutes, beginning about halfway through cooking. Keep the baste simmering so you aren't applying a cold liquid to the meat.

***Note:** To make rich beef stock, pour 2 14½-ounce cans of beef broth into a pan and simmer, with the cover off, until the broth is reduced to 2 cups.

Puerto Rican Barbecue Steak Sauce

This steak sauce will cover quite a few steaks—you won't use it all in one barbecue unless you are feeding the local softball team. So pour the amount you think you'll need into a bowl, and keep the rest in a jar. That way you won't contaminate the unused portion of the sauce with a brush that's gone from the raw meat to the sauce and back again.

Makes about 3 cups

1   cup peanut oil
¼   cup white vinegar
¼   cup Worcestershire sauce
1   large onion, minced
3   garlic cloves, pressed
2   fresh serrano chiles, seeded and minced
2   tablespoons dark brown sugar
1   tablespoon dry mustard powder
2   teaspoons minced fresh sage
1   teaspoon minced fresh thyme
1   teaspoon minced fresh parsley
1   teaspoon minced fresh chives
1   teaspoon hot pepper sauce
1   teaspoon sea salt
1   teaspoon black pepper
1   cup boiling water

Combine all the ingredients in a nonreactive saucepan, adding the boiling water last. Bring the mixture to a boil, stirring constantly. Reduce the heat to low, and simmer for 15 minutes. Use this sauce warm.

Use this sauce immediately, or store it in an airtight jar in the refrigerator for up to 1 week. Reheat it before using.

■ **How to Use It:** Brush steaks with the sauce before cooking and use as a basting sauce while grilling, basting frequently.

Hot Pepper Pork Mop

Two tablespoons of crushed red hot pepper give this mop a nice heat. If you want a milder mop, add only 1 tablespoon crushed red pepper.

Makes about 2 cups

1   12-ounce bottle of beer
1   cup ketchup (store-bought or homemade, see pages 238–40)
½ cup minced onions
2   tablespoons crushed red pepper
2   tablespoons brown sugar
1   lemon
2   garlic cloves, pressed
1   teaspoon seasoned salt

Cut the lemon in half and squeeze the juice out of each half, retaining the juice and the lemon halves. In a nonreactive saucepan, combine all of the ingredients, including the lemon juice and halves. Bring to a boil, stirring until well blended. Reduce the heat, and simmer for 30 minutes. Use warm.

Use this mop immediately, or store it in an airtight jar in the refrigerator for up to 2 weeks. Remove the lemon halves before storing the mop. Reheat it before using it.

■ **How to Use It:** This mop is great on ribs and pork butt. Don't be afraid to brush or mop it on frequently, so you can really taste the heat.

Start basting your barbecue after it has cooked for half of its projected cooking time. You want to give the rub a chance to form a crust on the meat before you start applying a baste.

Pork Mop

The flavors of this mop are a little more complex than those of the previous recipe, and the bacon adds extra smoke flavor.

Makes about 3 cups

¼ cup bacon drippings (grease)
½ cup minced onions
¼ cup minced celery
3 garlic cloves, pressed
2 cups apple cider or apple juice
1 cup tomato juice
¼ cup fresh lemon juice
2 tablespoons Worcestershire sauce
2 tablespoons brown sugar
1 tablespoon chili powder
2 teaspoons dry mustard powder
1 teaspoon ground thyme
1 teaspoon sea salt

Heat the bacon grease in a nonreactive saucepan over medium heat. Add the onions, celery, and garlic, and sauté until golden brown, about 5 minutes. Blend in the rest of the ingredients. Bring the mixture to a boil. Reduce the heat and simmer for 30 minutes. Use the mop warm.

Use the mop immediately, or store it in an airtight jar in the refrigerator for up to 1 week. Reheat it before using.

■ **How to Use It:** This is a good baste for grilled ribs. Brush the baste on both sides of ribs, and grill over hot coals, turning and basting often, until ribs are done.

Pork Baste

This baste has a slightly fruity flavor from the apple juice, which you can enhance by barbecuing over apple wood. This is a good basic mop for pork shoulder.

Makes about 2 cups

2   cups apple juice
¼   cup Worcestershire sauce
2   tablespoons white vinegar
1   tablespoon dry mustard powder
1   tablespoon brown sugar
1   bay leaf
2   teaspoons garlic salt
1   teaspoon ground ginger
½   teaspoon cayenne
¼   teaspoon ground cloves

Combine all of the ingredients in a nonreactive saucepan and bring the mixture to a boil. Reduce the heat and simmer, stirring occasionally, for 15 minutes. Use the baste warm.

Use the baste immediately, or store it in an airtight jar in the refrigerator for up to 1 month. Reheat it before using.

■ **How to Use It:** Starting halfway through the cooking time, baste or mop your pork frequently as it cooks over medium heat—about 6 hours cooking time for a 5- to 6-pound shoulder—or until your meat thermometer reaches 160°F. During the last hour of cooking, you may want to switch to a finishing sauce.

Nonreactive Cookware

Any time you are cooking with an acid—vinegar, wine, lemon juice, tomato products—you have to use cookware that won't react chemically with the acid and create an off flavor in the food. Aluminum, copper, and uncoated cast-iron cookware are the ones likely to react. Nonreactive cookware is usually made from stainless steel or enameled stainless steel. Nonstick cooking surfaces are usually nonreactive.

Remus Powers's Brazilian Citrus Mop and Finishing Sauce for Pork Shoulder

Remus Powers, a.k.a. Ardie Davis, Ph.B., Order of the Magic Mop, is the person responsible for starting the Ditty-Wa-Ditty Barbecue Sauce Contest, which is now the American Royal International Barbecue Sauce Contest, held the first weekend of October for commercial barbecue sauces from all over the world. Ardie is one of the top barbecue sauce experts in the world and author of his own cookbook. Maybe Ardie and I will coauthor a barbecue cookbook one of these days.

Makes about 4 cups

1   cup orange juice
1   cup fresh lemon juice
1   cup fresh lime juice
1   cup extra-virgin olive oil
3   tablespoons Dijon-style mustard
2   tablespoons The Baron's High Octane Seasoning (page 22)
1   tablespoon minced orange zest
1   tablespoon minced lemon zest

Put all of the ingredients in a nonreactive jar with a tight-fitting lid and shake until they are well blended.

This sauce is best used immediately, but it can be stored in the refrigerator in an airtight jar for up to 1 week. Reheat it before using.

■ **How to Use It:** Set aside 1 cup of the liquid for use as a finishing sauce. Use the rest of the sauce to baste or mop your pork frequently while it cooks over medium heat. Begin basting halfway through the cooking time, about 6 hours cooking time for a 5- to 6-pound shoulder, or until your meat thermometer reaches 160°F. Chop or pull the shoulder before serving. Sprinkle with the finishing sauce (the 1 cup you set aside), mix, and serve. This sauce makes a great marinade, too.

Pork and Bear Baste

Besides being a very good baste for pork, this mop is good on bear if you ever get a chance to barbecue some. Bear is very similar to pork; the old frontier settlers used to prize bear meat because it's the only wild game that has lots of fat in it.

Makes about 2 cups

1 cup stock or water
1 cup tomato juice
¼ cup Worcestershire sauce
¼ cup white vinegar
¼ cup ketchup (store-bought or homemade, pages 238–40)
2 lemons
1 medium onion, sliced thin
2 garlic cloves, pressed
1 bay leaf
2 tablespoons brown sugar
1 tablespoon chili powder
1 teaspoon dry mustard powder
1 teaspoon black pepper
1 teaspoon salt
½ teaspoon cayenne

Cut the lemons in half and squeeze the juice out of the halves, retaining the juice and the lemon halves. Combine all of the ingredients, including the lemon juice and halves, in a nonreactive saucepan, and bring to a boil over medium-high heat. Reduce the heat, and simmer, stirring occasionally, for 30 minutes. Use this baste warm.

Use the baste immediately, or store it in an airtight jar in the refrigerator for up to 1 month. Remove and discard the lemon halves before storing the baste. Reheat it before using.

■ **How to Use It:** Beginning halfway through the cooking time, baste or mop your pork shoulder or bear roast frequently while it cooks over medium heat—about 6 hours for a 5- to 6-pound piece of meat—or until your meat thermometer reaches 160°F. During the last hour of cooking, you may want to switch to a finishing sauce.

Tarragon Chicken Baste

East meets West in this baste. You've got your soy sauce from the East, and tarragon, an herb used a lot in France, representing the West. The soy gives the chicken a nice mahogany finish, and using butter in a baste gives it a richer flavor than oil.

Makes about 1 cup

- 1 cup (2 sticks) unsalted butter
- 2 tablespoons soy sauce
- 2 garlic cloves, pressed
- 1 teaspoon dried parsley flakes
- ½ teaspoon dried tarragon
- ½ teaspoon MSG (optional)

Combine all of the ingredients in a nonreactive saucepan over medium heat, and stir until the butter is melted. Simmer for 15 minutes, stirring occasionally. Keep the baste warm while it is being used.

Use the baste immediately, or store it in an airtight jar in the refrigerator for up to 1 week. Reheat it before using.

■ **How to Use It:** Beginning about halfway through the cooking time, brush onto a whole chicken every 10 to 15 minutes to keep it moist.

■ **Variation:** If tarragon isn't something you keep on hand, you can substitute basil or another herb.

Zesty Chicken Basting Sauce

This butter-based basting sauce is flavored with lemon and dill.

Makes about 1 cup

½ cup (1 stick) butter
¼ cup fresh lemon juice
2 tablespoons minced lemon zest
2 garlic cloves, pressed
1 tablespoon fresh parsley
1 teaspoon dried dill weed
1 teaspoon black pepper
1 teaspoon salt

> Your barbecued chicken is done if the juices run clear when the thigh is pierced.

Combine all of the ingredients in a nonreactive saucepan over medium heat, and stir until the butter is melted. Simmer for 15 minutes, stirring occasionally. Keep the baste warm while it is being used.

Use the sauce immediately, or store it in an airtight jar in the refrigerator for up to 1 week. Reheat it before using.

■ **How to Use It:** Beginning about halfway through the cooking time, brush onto a whole chicken every 10 to 15 minutes to keep it moist.

Chicken Baste au Naturel

This baste is made up mainly of chicken stock and fresh ingredients—thus the name, "Chicken Baste au Naturel."

Makes about 5 cups

1   quart chicken broth (store-bought or homemade,
    see page 142)
1¼ cups white wine
1   cup (2 sticks) butter
¼ cup olive oil
1   ounce fresh basil
2   garlic cloves, pressed
2   bay leaves
2   tablespoons fresh lemon juice
2   tablespoons fresh lime juice

Place the chicken broth in a nonreactive saucepan. Bring to a boil, and simmer until the broth is reduced by one third. Add the wine, butter, olive oil, basil, garlic, and bay leaves. Stir to blend the mixture well. Add the lemon and lime juices. Simmer for 10 minutes. Keep the baste warm during use, stirring it before you brush it on the chicken.

This baste is best when used right after it is made, but it can be stored in the refrigerator in an airtight jar for up to to 5 days. Reheat it before using.

■ How to Use It: When the chicken is half-done, begin brushing on this baste every 10 to 15 minutes to keep it moist.

If you are making a large quantity of a baste or mop, it is best to set some aside beforehand and refrigerate it for later use. Or, use the mop a half cup at a time, adding to it from your reserve as needed. This prevents any bacteria which may have been transferred from the raw meat to the basting brush from entering the reserve.

Barbados Barbecue Chicken Baste and Sauce

The combination of orange juice, lime juice, and soy sauce gives this baste its tropical appeal.

Makes about 2 1/2 cups

1½ cups strained orange juice
¼ cup strained fresh lime juice
¼ cup butter (½ stick), melted
¼ cup soy sauce
¼ cup clover honey
3 tablespoons minced fresh parsley
2 garlic cloves, pressed
1 teaspoon sea salt

Combine all of the ingredients in a nonreactive saucepan and heat over low heat. Stir until all the ingredients are blended well. Use the baste warm.

This baste is at its best freshly made. Unused portions will keep for up to 1 week in an airtight jar in the refrigerator. Reheat it before using.

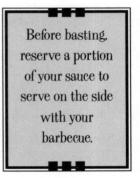

Before basting, reserve a portion of your sauce to serve on the side with your barbecue.

■ **How to Use It:** Brush the sauce on poultry before cooking, and use as a baste during cooking. Although I call this a chicken baste, the combination of duck and orange is always a winner, too.

■ **Variation:** Pineapple juice can replace the orange juice.

Beurre Blanc Basting Sauce for Fish

Beurre blanc means "white butter," and readers of French cookbooks will recognize this classic sauce made from wine and shallots, with butter whisked in at the end to create a velvety smooth texture.

Makes about 1 cup

½ cup minced shallots
2 garlic cloves, pressed
½ cup dry white wine
¼ cup fresh lemon juice
¼ cup fresh lime juice
2 tablespoons sugar
1½ cups (3 sticks) unsalted butter, cut into
    ½-inch-thick pieces, kept cold
1 teaspoon sea salt
1 teaspoon black pepper

In a nonreactive saucepan over medium heat, combine the shallots, garlic, wine, lemon juice, lime juice, and sugar. Cook, stirring, until the mixture begins to get thick and syrupy. Reduce the heat to low, and continue to stir. Be careful not to burn the shallots and garlic. Whisk the butter gently into the sauce—the secret of beurre blanc is to whisk in the butter carefully and slowly. Do not let the mixture come to a boil, or it will break and separate. When the butter has all been incorporated, add salt and pepper and keep warm. Use the sauce immediately.

■ **How to Use It:** This is a great baste for any grilled fish, and a good finishing sauce also. If you would like to use it as a finishing sauce, set aside half the sauce. Brush the rest on the fish before and during cooking. Serve the finishing sauce warm.

5

Barbecue Sauces

Barbecue sauce, barbecue sauce, barbecue sauce. Almost everyone of whom you ask, "What is barbecue?" says in reply, "It's the SAUCE!" You can ask the question anywhere in the nation, in barbecue country or not, and the answer is the same. Barbecue sauce *is* barbecue!

You can ask the same question of some of the old masters who are still around, and the new ones who are developing, and they will tell you a different story. They will say it's the cooker, it's the mop, it's the wood or charcoal, or it's their skill and technique. These are all very valid statements, but if you look behind the scenes, you will find all those masters have a finishing sauce of their own.

Personally, I think that real barbecue is in the seasoning. I believe that and I'm willing to back it up. I challenge my students by telling them that I will compete against them using their cooker and their sauce, with my barbecue seasoning, and I will win. That's how sure I am! Wait just one minute, oh Big One, don't you bottle and sell your own brand of barbecue sauce? If everything that you say is true, and the sauce doesn't make any difference, why go to the trouble of making your own? A good question, and to answer it we could go around in circles for another thirty to forty pages and still not get to a believable answer.

The best way I can put it into perspective is like this: Some people grew up with sauce, and some grew up without it. It's like someone asking me, "Why are you such a large person when I'm the size I am?" The simple answer is, that's the way each of us is. A person's taste for barbecue sauce seems almost as inevitable—if you grew up eating and liking barbecue sauce, you probably give it a great deal of importance. I myself grew up eating barbecue that had a simple salt and pepper rub, with a very good sauce used just as a glaze on the meat. The rest of the sauce was served on the side. You could use it, or leave it there, and I usually thought the meat was so tasty already, I didn't bother with the sauce. In my estimation, this is really the way this whole debate got started—people grew up accustomed to different things.

Barbecue sauce is used as a condiment, a dipping sauce, and a glaze. It is used to complement the flavor of your barbecue. In some cases, it is used to cover up the flavor of the barbecue and to give overcooked, dried barbecue some moisture. You don't need barbecue sauce, but your barbecue will be better with it than without it.

The world's best-selling barbecue sauce is Kraft, which was the first national brand of sauce introduced in America, by way of grocery stores in the 1950s. If you go to any supermarket in the country that carries barbecue sauce, you will find Kraft, Heinz, Hunts, and K. C. Masterpiece barbecue sauces, and they are all Kansas City–style sauces.

When most people talk about barbecue sauce, what they are really talking about is Kansas City–style sauce—tomato-based, sweet, and spicy, with some bite. It is also, as a general rule, thicker than most of the other regional sauces. Texas-style sauces are also tomato-based, but they are thinner in body, less sweet, and usually have molasses and Worcestershire sauce to give them distinction. Western-style Carolina sauces are found west of Raleigh. They are like Kansas City– and Texas-style sauces: tomato-based, primarily ketchup, with a lot of vinegar and sugar. They are on the order of a sweet-and-sour sauce. Eastern-style Carolina sauces are found east of Raleigh and on to the coast. These sauces are vinegar-based, with sugar, crushed red peppers, salt, and pepper for flavor. South Carolina and Georgia are where you get into the mustard-based sauces. One of the major barbecue styles that doesn't get much attention in cookbooks is Memphis-style barbecue sauce, which is based on a combination of tomato, mustard, and vinegar.

The more popular barbecue becomes, the more styles that emerge and become well defined, like Florida barbecue style, in which the sauces have a ketchup or tomato base with lemon and lime, vinegar, and butter. In various parts of the South, you'll find sauces that are a combination of the Carolina sauces. Owensboro, Kentucky, has a brown or black sauce that is usually applied to mutton, but can be used on pork and beef. California- or Western-style sauces are spirited, with a tomato or salsa base. Hawaiian-style barbecue is sweet-and-sour, with fruits and fruit juices. You

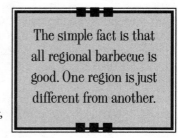

The simple fact is that all regional barbecue is good. One region is just different from another.

will also find Oriental sauces that are soy sauce– and peanut-based.

The American Royal Barbecue Association (at 1701 American Royal Court, Kansas City, Missouri 64102) puts on the International Invitational Contest for commercial sauces. It offers four categories for its sauces, Tomato, Mustard, Vinegar, and Fruit, with mild and hot divisions for each category. So, as you can see, there are a lot of different types of barbecue sauce out there.

Barbecue sauce can be utilized in a few different ways to add flavor to your barbecue. You can pour it on your meat or pool it on your plate for dipping. Or it can be painted on to glaze. To put a sauce glaze on your barbecue, pour some of your sauce into a separate bowl and dip your brush in it to paint or mop the sauce onto the meat during the last 30 to 45 minutes of cooking. Discard whatever sauce is left in the bowl. Be careful not to cook the glazed sauce for too long or over heat that is too intense, because it can caramelize and burn.

Master Class: Developing a Basic Kansas City–Style Barbecue Sauce

What makes it a good sauce? A good sauce seasons and enhances. It is not intended to hide or overpower or dominate! A sauce can give contrasting or complementary flavors. It can also add moisture, texture, and visual interest (color) to your barbecue. So let's develop a sauce that does all these things.

Kansas City pitmasters set the standard with their tomato-based, spicy, sweet sauce. Since this is the country's favorite style of barbecue sauce, we will work on developing one in this style.

STEP ONE: ANALYZE THE INGREDIENTS.

A Kansas City–style sauce has a tomato base, with ingredients that add sweetness, sour tang, and spices. Here's a rundown on the ingredients you can choose from.

Tomato

Ketchup: tomato paste, vinegar, sweetener, and spices
Tomato paste: tomato pulp reduced by slow cooking
Tomato purée: crushed or ground tomatoes in tomato sauce
Tomato sauce: tomato paste and water
Chili sauce: tomato purée with crushed tomatoes, onion,
    green pepper, and spices
Tomato soup: condensed tomato soup

Sweet	Sour
White sugar—cane or beet	Vinegar—cider, flavored,
Brown sugar—light or dark	or white
Honey	Wine
Molasses or sorghum	Beer
Corn syrup—light or dark	Citrus juices—lemon or lime
Corn sugar	
Date sugar	
Maple—sugar or syrup	

Other Liquids, for flavor or to thin the sauce

Booze
Coffee and tea
Fruit juices
Hoisin sauce
Horseradish
Jellies
Liquid smoke
Louisiana hot sauce
Mustard

Oil
Soft drinks
Soy sauce
Stock or broth
Tabasco sauce
Tomato juice
Water
Worcestershire sauce

Spices and Seasonings

Allspice
Anise
Barbecue spice
Basil
Bay leaf
Caraway
Celery—salt, ground, or seed
Cinnamon
Cloves
Coriander
Cumin
Curry powder
Dill weed
Dry mustard
Fennel
Garlic—salt, granulated, or powder
Ginger
Lemon zest
Mace

Marjoram
Mint
Nutmeg
Onion—salt, granulated, or or powder
Orange zest
Oregano
Parsley
Pepper—white, black, chili powder or seasoning, cayenne, or crushed red
Poultry seasoning
Rosemary
Sage
Savory
Tarragon
Thyme

Barbecue Sauce Work Sheet

Base	Product	Amount
Tomato:	_____	_____
	Notes: _____	
Mustard:	_____	_____
	Notes: _____	
Vinegar:	_____	_____
	Notes: _____	
Fruit/Soy:	_____	_____
	Notes: _____	
Nut/Fish:	_____	_____
	Notes: _____	
Sweets:	_____	_____
	Notes: _____	
Sours:	_____	_____
	Notes: _____	
Liquids:	_____	_____
	Notes: _____	
Spices:	_____	_____
	Notes: _____	
Miscellaneous:	_____	_____
	Notes: _____	

STEP TWO: DEFINE THE INGREDIENTS LIST FOR YOUR SAUCE.

We now have everything we need to develop our first barbecue sauce. On the development list we have tomato as the basic product, with 6 tomato products listed. Of the 6 products, I suggest that you use a keg, or 32-ounce bottle, of ketchup, so on the work sheet write 1 keg ketchup on the product line and 32 ounces on the amount line. Thirty-two ounces is a weight, not a volume measure. It may sound like a lot, but it will measure a scant 4 cups.

Of all the sweeteners, I suggest that we use one that will

add flavor, so that rules out white sugars and light syrups. I suggest 1 cup of sweetener. Let's use a ½ cup dark brown sugar and a ½ cup clover honey. Add the sugar and honey to the work sheet.

Next are sours. We are looking for a balance between sweet and sour in the final sauce, so we will use 1 cup of a sour ingredient, as we added 1 cup of sweet. Before we pick which sour ingredient to use, we need to look at the other ingredients we've chosen so far. Since ketchup already has vinegar in it, we need to add additional sour ingredients more sparingly, especially if you don't like a very sour flavor. Add the sour ingredient a little at a time. I suggest we use 1 cup of white vinegar. If you use a flavored vinegar, which is more expensive than white vinegar, I suggest that you add it during the last 10 minutes of cooking, so you don't cook off the flavor you are trying to achieve. Add 1 cup white vinegar to our work sheet, or, so that you will remember to add a little at a time, write it down in increments: ½ cup—¼ cup—¼ cup.

The other liquids are used to add to the flavor we want the sauce to have, or to thin the sauce. Three of the other liquids that are traditionally found in barbecue sauces are Worcestershire sauce, soy sauce, and liquid smoke. With reference to Worcestershire sauce or soy sauce, you can use one or the other or both to a total volume of ¼ cup. For our sauce, we are going to use both, so add 2 tablespoons Worcestershire sauce and 2 tablespoons soy sauce to your work sheet. An optional ingredient would be liquid smoke. This recipe can handle 1 tablespoon of liquid smoke. Add this to the list, if you like it in your sauce.

Basic traditional spices that are in a barbecue sauce are chili powder, black pepper, and salt, but any spice can be added, and you know what you like. This recipe can handle up to ¼ cup of chili powder, but since we don't know how much chili powder you like in your barbecue sauce, we will start with 2 tablespoons of chili powder. Write 2 tablespoons chili powder on the work sheet. The rule of thumb on black pepper is to use from half as much to the same amount of chili powder you used. I like the half rule, so enter 1 tablespoon of black pepper on the work sheet.

People eat first with their eyes.

Now I'm going to finish out the sauce with spices. To the work sheet, add 2 teaspoons rubbed sage, 1 teaspoon granulated garlic, 1 teaspoon ground allspice, 1 teaspoon salt (optional), ½ teaspoon ground cloves, ½ teaspoon cayenne (optional), and ¼ teaspoon ground mace.

This concludes the structure. Now let's put it together.

STEP THREE: MAKE THE SAUCE.

In a nonreactive saucepan, combine the brown sugar, chili powder, pepper, sage, garlic, allspice, salt, cloves, cayenne, and mace. Blend in ½ cup vinegar, the Worcestershire sauce, soy sauce, and liquid smoke if you are using it. Over medium-high heat, stir the mixture until the sugar and spices dissolve into the liquid. Add the honey and ketchup, and continue to stir.

Bring the mixture to a boil (be very careful because the ketchup will bubble and splatter). Reduce the heat, and simmer for 30 minutes, stirring occasionally. Taste the sauce and determine if you should blend in any more of the vinegar. Adjust any other seasonings to your taste.

Master Class Barbecue Sauce

Makes about 6 cups

½ cup dark brown sugar, packed
2 tablespoons chili powder
1 tablespoon black pepper
2 teaspoons rubbed sage
1 teaspoon ground allspice
1 teaspoon granulated garlic
1 teaspoon salt (optional)
½ teaspoon ground cloves
½ teaspoon cayenne (optional)
¼ teaspoon ground mace
1 cup white vinegar
½ cup clover honey
2 tablespoons Worcestershire sauce
2 tablespoons soy sauce
1 32-ounce bottle of ketchup

Combine all of the dry ingredients in a nonreactive saucepan.
Blend in the vinegar, honey, Worcestershire sauce, and soy
sauce. Bring the mixture to a boil. Stir in the ketchup, being
careful that the ketchup doesn't pop and splatter. Reduce the
heat and simmer for 30 minutes, stirring occasionally. Adjust
seasonings to taste.

Use the sauce warm or chilled. It will keep for several weeks
in an airtight jar in the refrigerator.

Balance the Flavors
The key to a good sauce is the
balance of its flavors. For
every sour note, add a sweet
one; for every hot flavor, add
something mild.

Ginger Barbecue Sauce

This is as close to my own personal sauce as I am willing to reveal. It's a classic Kansas City–style sauce, with a definite flavorprint of ginger. This recipe has never failed me.

Makes about 3 cups

2   cups tomato purée
1   cup tomato sauce
¼   cup brown sugar, packed
¼   cup wine vinegar
2   tablespoons minced candied ginger
2   tablespoons chili powder
2   tablespoons Worcestershire sauce
1   tablespoon minced dried onion
1   lemon, unpeeled, sliced thin
1   garlic clove, pressed
2   teaspoons black pepper
1   teaspoon celery salt
1   teaspoon dry mustard powder

Combine all of the ingredients in a nonreactive saucepan and blend well. Place over medium heat, and simmer for 20 minutes, stirring occasionally.

This sauce will keep for several weeks in an airtight jar in the refrigerator.

■ **How to Use It:** Use warm or chilled as a finishing sauce for pork of any kind. It is also a good sauce for pulled pork sandwiches. It makes a good glaze for poultry; start painting it on about 30 minutes before the end of the cooking time.

> Before slicing barbecued meat, let it rest for 20 to 30 minutes after taking it off the fire. It will be easier to slice, and the meat will be juicier.

Kansas City Barbecue Sauce

Here it is: the sauce from the sauce capital of the country. When people say "barbecue sauce," they mean "Kansas City barbecue sauce"—thick, tomato-rich, sweet, and spicy. The old-style recipes, like this one here, start with butter or bacon drippings, which makes them a little on the rich side.

Makes about 8 cups

½ cup (1 stick) unsalted butter
4 garlic cloves, pressed
1 cup minced onions
1 lemon, unpeeled, seeded and minced
1 32-ounce bottle ketchup
1 cup tomato juice
1 cup V-8 juice
1 cup brown sugar, packed
½ cup molasses
½ cup Worcestershire sauce
¼ cup chili powder
¼ cup white vinegar
2 tablespoons black pepper
1 teaspoon salt

Melt the butter in a nonreactive saucepan over medium heat. Add the garlic, onions, and lemon, and sauté until the onion is tender but not brown, about 4 minutes. Add the remaining ingredients. Bring the mixture to a boil, reduce the heat and simmer, stirring occasionally, for 1 to 1½ hours or until the sauce has thickened.

Use the sauce warm or chilled. It will keep for 2 weeks in an airtight jar in the refrigerator.

■ How to Use It: Glaze this sauce on your chicken or pork ribs about 30 minutes before the end of the cooking time, and you will be the neighborhood barbecue "King." It's also really good as a topping for hamburgers.

Kansas City Rib Doctor Chicken Sauce

The Kansas City Rib Doctor was one of my first students—he is an excellent barbecuer, who has won the Kansas State Rib Championship. His team, which included his wife, who is a nurse, wore hospital scrubs for their uniforms, and he's been called the Kansas City Rib Doctor ever since. This sauce, a nice basic one, proves that ribs aren't the Rib Doctor's only specialty.

Makes about 3 cups

- ⅓ cup (⅔ stick) unsalted butter
- 2 tablespoons grated onion
- 4 garlic cloves, pressed
- 1 6-ounce can tomato paste
- 2 cups cider vinegar
- 1 cup vegetable oil
- ¼ cup Worcestershire sauce
- 1 tablespoon seasoned salt
- 1 tablespoon Louisiana-style hot sauce

Melt the butter in a nonreactive saucepan over medium heat. Add the onion and garlic, and sauté until soft but not browned, about 3 minutes. Add the rest of the ingredients and blend well. Bring the mixture to a boil, then reduce the heat and simmer for 15 minutes, stirring occasionally.

This sauce will keep for 2 weeks in an airtight jar in the refrigerator.

■ How to Use It: Use this sauce warm or chilled. It's a good basting sauce and finishing sauce for chicken. It also works well as a chicken marinade.

Sweet Kansas City Barbecue Sauce

This is a sweet all-purpose barbecue sauce, with some bite. I think it can use about a tablespoon of crushed red pepper, but start with a teaspoon and increase it from there—you may think a tablespoon is too much.

Makes about 10 cups

2   12-ounce cans tomato paste
2½ cups water
1   cup molasses
1   cup dark corn syrup
1   cup clover honey
1   cup brown sugar, packed
1   cup cider vinegar
¼   cup Worcestershire sauce
2   tablespoons soy sauce
2   tablespoons chili powder
2   tablespoons granulated garlic
1   tablespoon black pepper
1   tablespoon granulated onion
1   tablespoon rubbed sage
1   tablespoon salt
1   tablespoon liquid smoke
2   teaspoons cayenne
½   teaspoon ground bay leaf
1 to 3 teaspoons crushed red pepper

You are never too young or too old to enjoy a barbecue contest.

Combine all of the ingredients in a large, nonreactive saucepan. Bring the mixture to a boil, stirring to blend the ingredients well. Reduce the heat and simmer for about 30 minutes, stirring occasionally to make sure the sauce on the bottom of the pan does not scorch.

This sauce will keep for several weeks in an airtight jar in the refrigerator.

■ **How to Use It:** Use this sauce warm or chilled, as a dipping sauce with any kind of chicken or pork. You don't want to glaze with it, as the high sugar content will cause it to burn too quickly.

Tried-and-True Barbecue Sauce

You were wondering what to do with all that Master Barbecue Spice you mixed up after reading chapter 1? Well, here is your chance to use it. This is a good all-purpose barbecue sauce made with a tomato sauce base. You can probably whip this up with ingredients you have on hand, any time you hear the call of the "Q". This is very similar to my family's barbecue sauce, which I started barbecuing with when I was nine years old.

Makes about 2 1/2 cups

- 2   tablespoons Master Barbecue Spice (page 21)
- 1   tablespoon chili seasoning
- 1   teaspoon black pepper
- 1   teaspoon ground ginger
- ½   teaspoon garlic powder
- ½   teaspoon salt
- 1   15-ounce can tomato sauce
- ½   cup dark brown sugar, packed
- ¼   cup white vinegar

Combine the Barbecue Spice, chili seasoning, black pepper, ginger, garlic powder, and salt in a nonreactive saucepan. Blend in the tomato sauce, brown sugar, and vinegar. Make sure the tomato sauce is mixed in well. Bring the mixture to a boil. Reduce the heat, and simmer for about 10 minutes, stirring occasionally.

Or, instead of cooking, combine the ingredients, blend them well, and set the mixture aside for 2 to 3 hours before using.

This sauce will keep for several weeks in an airtight jar in the refrigerator.

■ **How to Use It:** Use this sauce warm or chilled. It is a good all-purpose sauce you can use to finish just about any meat—beef, pork, lamb, chicken, turkey, duck, you name it. Just paint it on warm about 30 minutes before the end of the cooking time—or serve it as a dipping sauce alongside the meal.

A Little Southern Barbecue Sauce

Not all southern barbecue sauces feature tomato bases, but many have a sweet and sour flavor combination. This one has both elements.

Makes about 3¹/2 cups

1   6-ounce can tomato paste
¼   cup ketchup (store-bought or homemade, pages 238–40)
2   cups water
½   cup brown sugar, packed
¼   cup fresh lemon juice
¼   cup Worcestershire sauce
2   tablespoons cider vinegar
1   small onion, minced
2   garlic cloves, pressed
1   teaspoon ground allspice
1   teaspoon salt
1   teaspoon black pepper

Combine all of the ingredients in a nonreactive saucepan. Bring the mixture to a boil. Reduce the heat, and simmer for 30 minutes, stirring occasionally.

This sauce will keep for several weeks in an airtight jar in the refrigerator.

■ **How to Use It:** This being a Southern-style sauce, it was made to be used with pork—as a baste or finishing sauce. It's great on barbecued ribs. Use it warm or chilled.

> **Too Much of a Good Thing**
> Don't overdo a favorite ingredient. Just because a little of it tastes good in a sauce doesn't mean that a lot will taste better. When adding spices, add a half a teaspoon at a time and keep tasting as you go.

Uncle John's Great Southern Barbecue Sauce

Uncle John is one of my long-gone relatives. But his sauces have been passed down from generation to generation. The pickle and lemon are truly distinctive touches. Ol' Uncle John probably put this one on pork shoulder, the centerpiece of Southern-style pit-in-the-ground barbecue. You can use it on any cut of pork, whether pit-smoked or grilled.

Makes about 6¼ cups

- ½ cup (1 stick) unsalted butter
- ¼ cup minced onion
- ¼ cup minced green bell pepper
- 1 garlic clove, pressed
- 2 cups chili sauce
- 2 cups ketchup (store-bought or homemade, pages 238–40)
- 1 cup cider vinegar
- ½ cup brown sugar, packed
- ¼ cup Worcestershire sauce
- 2 tablespoons minced sour pickle
- 1 lemon, unpeeled, sliced

Place the butter in a large nonreactive saucepan and melt it over medium heat. Add the onion, green pepper, and garlic and sauté until they are soft, about 7 to 8 minutes. Add the chili sauce, ketchup, vinegar, brown sugar, Worcestershire sauce, pickle, and lemon. Bring the mixture to a boil. Reduce the heat and simmer for 45 minutes, stirring occasionally.

This sauce will keep for up to 2 weeks in an airtight jar in the refrigerator, but fish out the lemon slices after a day or so, or the lemon will overpower the sauce.

■ How to Use It: Use this sauce warm, as a finishing sauce for pork of any kind. Paint it on about 30 minutes before the end of the cooking time. It's also a good spreading sauce for pulled pork sandwiches. At the table, you can serve it warm or chilled.

Sweet and Tangy Barbecue Sauce

Here's another good all-purpose barbecue sauce—a model of balanced flavors. It has sweetness from fruit juice, brown sugar, molasses, and honey, tang from fruity cider vinegar, and just enough heat from the combination of chili powder, cayenne, and mustard. Lemon powder adds a little mystery—the flavor that makes you stop for a minute and ask, "Yes, but what is that other flavor?" as you help yourself to more.

Makes about 3 cups

2   tablespoons butter
1   small onion, minced
2   cups ketchup (store-bought or homemade, pages 238–40)
¼   cup water
¼   cup apple juice
¼   cup cider vinegar
¼   cup Worcestershire sauce
2   tablespoons brown sugar
2   tablespoons molasses
2   tablespoons clover honey
2   teaspoons dry mustard powder
1   teaspoon chili seasoning
1   teaspoon garlic powder
1   teaspoon cayenne
1   teaspoon lemon powder*

Melt the butter in a nonreactive saucepan over medium heat. Add the onion, and sauté until the onion is soft, but not browned, about 3 minutes. Add the remaining ingredients to the saucepan, stirring to blend them well, and bring to a boil. Reduce the heat and simmer for 30 minutes, stirring occasionally to avoid scorching the sauce at the bottom of the pan.

This sauce will keep for several weeks in an airtight jar in the refrigerator.

■ **How to Use It:** This is an outstanding pork barbecue sauce and is also good on chicken. Use the sauce warm, as a finishing sauce or glaze. Or serve it at the table, warm or chilled.

*Note: For information on lemon powder, see page 30.

Memphis-Style Barbecue Sauce

When you say Memphis barbecue sauce, you say pork! This sauce is a classic—you've got your ketchup, your mustard, your brown sugar, your vinegar, and your spices. The pepper, chili powder, and Tabasco make this sauce a lively one.

Makes about 5 cups

1	32-ounce bottle ketchup
1	cup brown sugar, packed
½	cup prepared yellow mustard
½	cup cider vinegar
¼	cup chili powder
2	tablespoons liquid smoke
1	tablespoon black pepper
1	tablespoon Worcestershire sauce
1	tablespoon garlic salt
2	teaspoons Tabasco sauce
1	teaspoon celery salt

Combine all of the ingredients in a nonreactive saucepan, and blend well. Place the mixture over medium heat and simmer for 30 minutes, stirring occasionally.

This sauce will keep for several weeks in an airtight jar in the refrigerator.

■ **How to Use It:** Use this sauce warm or chilled, as a finishing sauce for pork of any kind. It's especially tasty on a pulled pork sandwich.

Down-Home Barbecue Sauce

Down home is Memphis—the home of sauce made from toma-toes, mustard, and vinegar. Compared to the previous sauce, this one has a little less heat but more in the way of aromatic spices.

Makes about 5¼ cups

2   tablespoons chili powder
2   tablespoons black pepper
2   teaspoons ground cinnamon
1   teaspoon ground allspice
1   teaspoon salt
½   teaspoon cayenne
1   32-ounce bottle ketchup
½   cup prepared yellow mustard
½   cup cider vinegar
1   cup brown sugar
2   tablespoons Worcestershire sauce
2   tablespoons soy sauce
1   tablespoon liquid smoke

Barbecue and barbecue sauce make great personalized gifts.

Combine the chili powder, black pepper, cinnamon, allspice, salt, and cayenne in a nonreactive saucepan. Blend in the ketchup, mustard, vinegar, brown sugar, Worcestershire sauce, soy sauce, and liquid smoke. Make sure that the ketchup is blended in well. Bring the mixture to a boil. Reduce the heat and simmer for about 30 minutes, stirring occasionally.

This sauce will keep for several weeks in an airtight jar in the refrigerator.

■ **How to Use It:** This is an outstanding pork barbecue sauce and is also good on chicken. Use the sauce warm or chilled, as a finishing sauce or dipping sauce. This is a great sauce for a pig sandwich—pulled pork on a bun or bread, topped with cole slaw.

Mild Memphis Barbecue Sauce

Don't mistake "mild" for "boring." This sauce doesn't have much heat, but it's got a nice tang from the vinegar and mustard, and plenty of flavor besides.

Makes about 3 cups

1   12-ounce can tomato paste
1   cup white vinegar
½   cup water
½   cup prepared yellow mustard
¼   cup dark brown sugar, packed
⅓   cup Worcestershire sauce
1   tablespoon butter
½   cup minced onions
2   teaspoons black pepper
1   teaspoon granulated garlic
1   teaspoon salt
½   teaspoon cayenne

Combine all of the ingredients in a large nonreactive saucepan, and blend well. Bring to a quick boil, then reduce the heat and simmer for 10 to 15 minutes. Serve warm or chilled.

This sauce will keep for several weeks in an airtight jar in the refrigerator.

■ **How to Use It:** Besides using this sauce with pork, try it as a finishing sauce for chicken or turkey. Begin applying the sauce about 30 minutes before the end of the cooking time.

■ **Variation:** You can mellow the sauce a bit by switching from white vinegar to cider vinegar. Or if you want a little more punch, add a tablespoon of chili powder or Master Barbecue Spice (page 21).

Granddad's Barbecue Sauce

This is one of the barbecue sauces that I grew up on, and I think it's very good. The flavors are simple and direct.

Makes about 5 cups

3   cups ketchup (store-bought or homemade, pages 238–40)
1   cup prepared yellow mustard
½   cup white vinegar
½   cup brown sugar, packed
2   tablespoons Louisiana-style hot sauce
1   tablespoon liquid smoke
2   tablespoons chili powder
1   tablespoon black pepper

Mix all of the ingredients thoroughly in a nonreactive bowl.

This sauce will keep for several weeks in an airtight jar in the refrigerator.

■ **How to Use It:** This sauce is good with any type of pork. Granddad was partial to this sauce for finishing ribs. Begin painting it on the meat about 30 minutes before the end of cooking. Or serve it as a table sauce.

■ **Variations:** For a hotter sauce, double the amount of Louisiana-style hot sauce.

Note: This sauce can easily be altered into Granddad's Basting Sauce. If you want to use it as a basting sauce for ribs, thin it out by adding ¼ cup apple juice or water, and ¼ cup of white vinegar.

A common cooking substitution for 1 cup of barbecue sauce is 1 cup ketchup plus 2 tablespoons Worcestershire sauce.

Smoky Barbecue Sauce

This is a pretty classic Texas-style barbecue sauce—similar to the Kansas City sauces, but sweetened with molasses. The smoky flavor comes from liquid smoke.

Makes about 7½ cups

2 tablespoons chili powder
1 tablespoon black pepper
2 teaspoons ground coriander
2 teaspoons dry mustard powder
1 teaspoon ground ginger
1 teaspoon granulated garlic
1 teaspoon cayenne
½ teaspoon ground nutmeg
1 32-ounce bottle ketchup
1 6-ounce can tomato paste
1 cup white vinegar
1 cup molasses
¼ cup Worcestershire sauce
2 tablespoons liquid smoke

Combine the chili powder, black pepper, coriander, mustard, ginger, garlic, cayenne, and nutmeg in a nonreactive saucepan. Blend in the ketchup, tomato paste, vinegar, molasses, Worcestershire sauce, and liquid smoke. Make sure that the tomato paste is blended in well. Bring the mixture to a boil. Reduce the heat and simmer for about 30 minutes, stirring occasionally.

This sauce will keep for several weeks in an airtight jar in the refrigerator.

■ How to Use It: Use the sauce warm or chilled. This is a good all-purpose barbecue sauce for brisket, ribs, chicken, or pork. The smoky flavor makes it ideal to use on quick-cooking grill items, such as steaks, chicken parts, and pork tenderloins.

A Favorite Barbecue Sauce

I'm partial to the flavor of bacon in a barbecue sauce, so this sauce is one of my favorites.

Makes about 3 cups

¼ cup bacon drippings (grease)
1 large onion, minced
2 garlic cloves, pressed
1 green bell pepper, seeded and minced
½ cup ketchup (store-bought or homemade, pages 238–40)
1 6-ounce can tomato paste
¾ cup water
½ cup brown sugar, packed
¼ cup white vinegar
¼ cup Worcestershire sauce
2 tablespoons chili powder
1 tablespoon black pepper
2 teaspoons dry mustard powder
1 teaspoon salt
1 teaspoon cayenne

Melt the bacon drippings in a large nonreactive saucepan. Add the onion, garlic, and green pepper and sauté until tender, but not browned, about 4 minutes. Add the rest of the ingredients, and stir to blend well. Bring the mixture to a boil. Reduce the heat and simmer for 1 hour, stirring occasionally.

This sauce will keep for up to 2 weeks in an airtight jar in the refrigerator.

■ **How to Use It:** Use this sauce warm, to glaze beef, pork, chicken, and lamb. It also makes a fine spread for a pulled pork sandwich or a burger.

Fire Chief's Delight

If you like a hot sauce you should like this one—we are talking serious heat here. This barbecue sauce can, and will, open up your smokestacks, but it is good.

Makes about 8 cups

- ¼ cup (½ stick) butter
- 1 medium onion, minced
- 1 medium green bell pepper, minced
- 4 cups ketchup (store-bought or homemade, pages 238–40)
- 2 cups water
- 1 cup white vinegar
- ½ cup dark brown sugar, packed
- ½ cup molasses
- ¼ cup Worcestershire sauce
- ¼ cup chili powder
- 2 tablespoons black pepper
- 1 tablespoon crushed red pepper
- 1 tablespoon cayenne
- 1 tablespoon dry mustard powder
- 2 teaspoons ground allspice
- 1 teaspoon ground cloves
- 1 teaspoon salt
- ½ teaspoon ground jalapeño
- ¼ teaspoon ground nutmeg

Melt the butter in a nonreactive saucepan over medium-high heat. Add the onion and green pepper and sauté until they are soft and tender, but not browned, about 4 minutes. Add the rest of the ingredients, and bring the mixture to a boil. Reduce the heat and simmer for 30 to 45 minutes, stirring occasionally.

This sauce will keep for up to 2 weeks in an airtight jar in the refrigerator.

■ **How to Use It:** Nice hot sauce like this is perfect for brisket—as fine a finishing sauce as you could ask for. But don't hesitate to try it on chicken and pork, too. Serve the sauce warm or chilled, as a dipping sauce.

Granddad's Hotshot Barbecue Sauce

This is one of the barbecue sauces I grew up on, and I think it's very good. It's a little bit hot, but not so hot that you can't taste your food. When our family would have a big get-together, my dad would do the barbecuing—he was the master barbecuer. My mother would make our sauce, which is on the sweet side, and granddad would bring the hot sauce.

Makes about 2¹/2 cups

- 1   15-ounce can tomato sauce
- ½   cup brown sugar, packed
- ⅓   cup cider vinegar
- ¼   cup Worcestershire sauce
- 1   tablespoon fresh lemon juice
- 1   tablespoon chili powder
- 2   teaspoons honey mustard
- 2   teaspoons cayenne
- 1   teaspoon crushed red pepper
- 1   teaspoon ground ginger
- 1   teaspoon onion powder
- 1   teaspoon garlic powder

Combine all of the ingredients in a nonreactive saucepan over medium-high heat. Bring the mixture to a boil. Reduce the heat, and simmer for 30 minutes, stirring occasionally.

This sauce will keep for several weeks in an airtight jar in the refrigerator.

■ **How to Use It:** Granddad was a pork man from way back, so this sauce is excellent on ribs and pork shoulder. But it also makes a fine finishing sauce for beef and chicken, too. Use warm or chilled, as a dipping sauce.

Redhook Barbecue Sauce

This sauce is a direct result of one of the Pitmaster classes I gave at the Redhook Ale Brewery in Woodinville, Washington. Every March, Bob Lyon, Ph.B., the secretary and one of the founders of the Pacific Northwest Barbecue Association, teams up with me to give this class. The beer in this sauce gives it a pleasant, slightly bitter tang.

Makes about 6 cups

- 4 cups ketchup (store-bought or homemade, pages 238–40)
- ½ cup chili sauce
- ½ cup brown sugar, packed
- ½ cup Redhook Ale (or other premium beer or ale)
- ½ cup red wine vinegar
- ⅓ cup fresh lemon juice
- ¼ cup vegetable oil
- 3 tablespoons A.1. steak sauce
- 2 tablespoons dry mustard powder
- 2 tablespoons soy sauce
- 2 teaspoons coarsely ground black pepper
- 2 teaspoons sea salt
- 1 teaspoon crushed red pepper

Combine all of the ingredients in a nonreactive saucepan, and blend well. Bring the mixture to a boil. Reduce the heat and simmer for 20 minutes, stirring occasionally.

This sauce will keep for up to 2 weeks in an airtight jar in the refrigerator.

■ **How to Use It:** This sauce is especially good as a finishing sauce on grilled shrimp and chicken. Serve it warm or chilled.

Carolyn Wells's Southern Comfort Barbecue Sauce

Carolyn Wells, Ph.B., is the "First Lady of Barbecue." She is the executive director of the world's largest barbecue society, the Kansas City Barbecue Society, and one of its founders. She is Secretary of the NBBQA, the National Barbecue Association. She is the United States liaison to the World Barbecue Association (WBQA), located in Zurich, Switzerland. She is also on the American Royal Barbecue Contest Advisory Board, which organizes the world's largest barbecue contest. In her spare time, Carolyn has written several barbecue cookbooks. This is one of her sauces.

Makes about 6 cups

- 1 cup prepared yellow mustard
- ½ cup Southern Comfort liquor
- ½ cup molasses
- ½ cup cider vinegar
- ¼ cup dark brown sugar, packed
- ¼ cup Worcestershire sauce
- 2 tablespoons fresh lemon juice
- 2 tablespoons soy sauce
- 2 teaspoons granulated garlic
- 2 teaspoons black pepper
- 1 teaspoon crushed red pepper
- 1 teaspoon cayenne
- 1 teaspoon salt
- 1 28-ounce bottle ketchup

Combine all of the ingredients, except the ketchup, in a nonreactive saucepan over medium heat, stirring to dissolve all of the ingredients. Add the ketchup and bring to a boil. Reduce the heat and simmer for 15 minutes, stirring occasionally.

This sauce will keep for several weeks in an airtight jar in the refrigerator.

■ How to Use It: This sauce says "pork" all over it, but it can be used as a finishing sauce on beef or chicken, as well. Begin applying it to the meat about 30 minutes before the end of the cooking time. Or serve it warm or chilled, as a table sauce.

Well-Married Barbecue Sauce

I have given this recipe to several people that are looking for a different and interesting barbecue sauce. But when I give it to them, they say, "How can this be very good? It has everything but the spice shelf in it!" I understand their skepticism, but as I tell them, all of the ingredients marry well to make a great sauce.

Makes about 9 cups

- 1 28-ounce bottle ketchup
- 1½ cups cider vinegar
- 1½ cups brown sugar, packed
- 1 12-ounce bottle chili sauce
- 1 12-ounce can ginger ale
- ½ cup fresh lemon juice
- ½ cup steak sauce
- ⅓ cup prepared yellow mustard
- ¼ cup Worcestershire sauce
- 2 tablespoons black pepper
- 2 tablespoons vegetable oil
- 1 tablespoon soy sauce
- 1 teaspoon dry mustard powder
- 2 garlic cloves, pressed
- ¼ teaspoon Louisiana-style hot sauce

Combine all of the ingredients in a nonreactive bowl, and blend well.

This sauce will keep for up to 1 month in an airtight jar in the refrigerator.

■ **How to Use It:** Use this sauce warm or chilled. It is a good finishing sauce for any cut of beef.

All-Purpose Texas Barbecue Sauce

Texas barbecue usually means beef, but that's not always the case. Texans barbecue everything—including goat—and do it very well. This is a good all-purpose barbecue sauce.

Makes about 7 cups

4   cups ketchup (store-bought or homemade, pages 238–40)
½   cup white vinegar
½   cup vegetable oil
½   cup molasses
½   cup clover honey
½   cup flat beer
2   tablespoons Worcestershire sauce
2   tablespoons fresh lemon juice
1   tablespoon black pepper
2   teaspoons garlic salt
1   teaspoon onion salt
1   teaspoon cayenne

Combine all of the ingredients in a nonreactive saucepan, and bring to a boil. Reduce the heat and simmer, stirring occasionally, for 1 to 2 hours or until the sauce reaches the desired thickness.

This sauce will keep for several weeks in an airtight jar in the refrigerator.

■ **How to Use It:** Serve warm or chilled. You can use this sauce on just about anything you want from beef steaks to chickens. As a glaze, start applying it about 30 minutes before the end of the cooking time.

Doubling Recipes

There's no problem with doubling recipes, even tripling recipes, once you're on to a good thing. But that's all the more reason to take careful notes when you make up your own sauce. You don't want to end up with a large quantity of a mediocre sauce.

Smoky Texas Barbecue Sauce

This sauce starts with onions cooking in meat drippings. The best way to do this is to render, or cook down, brisket trimmings to get the ¼ cup of beef drippings. Another procedure would be to barbecue your brisket and render the smoked trimmings; it adds a whole new dimension to your sauce. If you absolutely have to, you can substitute butter or oil, but the flavor won't be the same.

Makes about 2 cups

- ¼ cup meat drippings
- ¼ cup minced onion
- 2 cups ketchup (store-bought or homemade, pages 238–40)
- ¼ cup Worcestershire sauce
- ¼ cup molasses
- 1 tablespoon Tabasco sauce
- 1 teaspoon garlic salt
- ¼ cup fresh lemon juice

Heat the meat drippings in a nonreactive saucepan over medium heat. Add the onion and sauté until soft and translucent, about 5 minutes. Add the rest of the ingredients, and stir to blend well. Bring the mixture to a boil, then reduce the heat and simmer for 30 to 45 minutes.

This sauce will keep for about 1 week in an airtight jar in the refrigerator.

■ **How to Use It:** Use this sauce on beef—any cut, any kind—it is a very good finishing sauce. It's also a good table sauce. Serve it warm or chilled.

Texas-Style Brisket Barbecue Sauce

Texas is famous for its barbecued brisket, and this is the kind of sauce that put the meat on the map. Why brisket is the meat of choice for barbecue has to do with the fact that brisket is so tough and fatty. Only long, slow cooking will turn it into something worth eating. With a finishing sauce like this one, barbecued brisket is indeed worth eating.

Makes about 7 cups

- ½ cup (1 stick) butter
- 2 cups minced onions
- 4 garlic cloves, pressed
- 2 cups ketchup (store-bought or homemade, pages 238–40)
- 2 cups chili sauce
- 1 cup brown sugar, packed
- ½ cup fresh lemon juice
- ¼ cup red wine vinegar
- 2 tablespoons Worcestershire sauce
- 1 tablespoon liquid smoke
- 1 tablespoon prepared yellow mustard
- 2 teaspoons salt
- 2 teaspoons black pepper
- 1 teaspoon cayenne

Heat the butter in a large nonreactive saucepan over medium-high heat. Add the onions and garlic and sauté for 2 to 3 minutes, until just soft. Pour in the ketchup and chili sauce, and blend in well. Add the rest of the ingredients. Bring the mixture to a boil, then reduce the heat and simmer for 30 to 45 minutes, stirring occasionally.

This sauce will keep for up to 2 weeks in an airtight jar in the refrigerator.

■ How to Use It: Begin applying the sauce warm to barbecuing brisket, about 30 minutes before the end of the cooking time.

Maple Barbecue Sauce

This sauce has the same tomato base of a Kansas City sauce, but it is more of a Northeastern sauce; the maple extract gives it a very distinctive flavor.

Makes about 1 cup

- 1 cup tomato purée
- 1 tablespoon fresh lemon juice
- 1 tablespoon sugar
- 2 teaspoons Worcestershire sauce
- 1 teaspoon celery salt
- 1 teaspoon steak sauce
- 1 teaspoon liquid smoke
- ½ teaspoon granulated onion
- ¼ teaspoon cayenne
- ⅛ teaspoon maple extract

Combine all the ingredients in a nonreactive bowl, and mix well. Let the mixture rest for about 2 hours before using it, to allow the flavors to blend.

This sauce will keep for up to 2 weeks in an airtight jar in the refrigerator.

■ **How to Use It:** Serve this sauce warm or chilled. It is good on any barbecue, but the delicate flavor of maple works especially well with chicken and seafood, particularly shrimp. You can use this as a finishing sauce over direct heat on the grill; because of its lower sugar content, it will not burn as some of the other sauces will.

Tomato Soup Barbecue Sauce

Some people think you can't get good flavor out of a can, but that's just not so. This is one of my favorite sauces for chicken. The tomato becomes a background for all of the sweet, sour, and tangy flavors to work against.

Makes about 3 cups

- 2 tablespoons vegetable oil
- ½ cup minced onions
- 1 10½-ounce can condensed tomato soup
- ½ cup water
- ½ cup brown sugar, packed
- ½ cup white vinegar
- ¼ cup Worcestershire sauce
- ¼ cup paprika
- 2 tablespoons chili powder
- 2 tablespoons black pepper
- 1 tablespoon liquid smoke
- 2 teaspoons dry mustard powder
- 1 teaspoon salt
- ½ teaspoon ground rosemary
- 1 garlic clove, pressed

> A chicken is for barbecue what canvas is for a painter.

Heat the oil in a large nonreactive saucepan over medium heat. Add the onion, and sauté it until soft, but not brown, about 4 minutes. Add the rest of the ingredients, and blend well. Bring the mixture to a boil, reduce the heat, and simmer for 5 to 10 minutes, stirring occasionally.

This sauce will keep for several weeks in an airtight jar in the refrigerator.

■ **How to Use It:** Serve this sauce warm or chilled. You can't do any better than this as a dipping or finishing sauce for chicken, but it works well with pork, too.

Western Barbecue Steak Sauce

This is a very good barbecue sauce! When I make it, I like to add more horseradish, just because I really like its flavor.

Makes about 2¹/4 cups

- ½ cup bacon drippings (grease)
- ½ cup minced onions
- 1 garlic clove, pressed
- 2 bay leaves
- 2 cups ketchup (store-bought or homemade, pages 238–40)
- ⅓ cup fresh lemon juice
- 2 tablespoons Worcestershire sauce
- 1 tablespoon prepared horseradish, or more to taste
- 1 teaspoon seasoned salt
- ½ teaspoon white pepper

Melt the bacon drippings in a large nonreactive saucepan over medium heat. Add the onions, garlic, and bay leaves, and sauté for 3 to 4 minutes, until the onions are soft but not brown. Add the rest of the ingredients, bring to a boil, and simmer for 30 minutes. Remove and discard the bay leaves. Let the sauce stand for 4 to 5 hours so the flavors will blend.

This sauce will keep for about 1 week in an airtight jar in the refrigerator.

■ **How to Use It:** Horseradish and beef are a flavor combination you can't argue with. Use this as a finishing sauce or condiment, with brisket or grilled steak.

Bob Lyon's Cajun Barbecue Sauce

Bob Lyon, Ph.B., is a major force behind the continuation and great success of the Pacific Northwest Barbecue Association. Bob will be the co-author of my next barbecue cookbook. He is a food writer and correspondent for *National Barbecue News,* and is editor and publisher of *Drippings from the Pit.*

This sauce is a tan color, not red the way you may think sauce should be. You can add red food coloring or some paprika—if you think you really need the sauce to be red.

Makes about 6 cups

¼ cup flat Redhook Ale (or other premium beer or ale)
2 teaspoons onion flakes
2 teaspoons granulated garlic
1½ teaspoons black pepper
½ teaspoon white pepper
½ teaspoon cayenne
1 tablespoon seasoned salt
2 tablespoons pork fat (lard)
1 medium onion, diced
½ pound smoked (barbecued) pork, chopped
½ cup chopped pecans
4 garlic cloves, pressed
2 cups beef stock
12 ounces chili sauce
¼ cup orange juice
2 tablespoons fresh lemon juice
1 cup clover honey
1½ teaspoons habanero pepper sauce
¼ cup (½ stick) butter

In a large glass measuring cup, combine the beer with the onion flakes, granulated garlic, black pepper, white pepper, cayenne, and seasoned salt. Set the mixture aside.

In a nonreactive saucepan, melt the pork fat over medium heat. Add the onion, and sauté until it is translucent, about 4 minutes. Add the chopped pork and cook, stirring for about 2 minutes. Add the beer mixture and the rest of the ingredients, except the butter. Simmer the sauce for 2 hours over medium to low heat, stirring occasionally. Whisk in the butter, and blend well.

Cool this sauce before using. This sauce will keep for up to 1 week in an airtight jar in the refrigerator.

■ **How to Use It:** This is a pretty unique sauce with pork, pecans, garlic, and beer all in the ingredients list. I serve this as a table sauce so that the flavors don't get lost.

Carolina Mustard Sauce

South Carolina is where you find mustard sauces, with no tomatoes to balance them out. If you like mustard—or you just want to explore this type of "Q"—this is a good sauce to try. It will give you a completely different perspective on barbecue.

Makes about 2 cups

2	tablespoons vegetable oil
½	cup minced onions
1	cup prepared yellow mustard
½	cup fresh lemon juice
¼	cup brown sugar, packed
¼	cup white vinegar
1	teaspoon celery seeds
1	teaspoon salt

Heat the oil in a medium-size nonreactive saucepan over medium heat. Add the onions and sauté until translucent, about 3 to 4 minutes. Add the rest of the ingredients, and blend them well. Bring the mixture to a boil, then reduce the heat and simmer for 15 to 20 minutes, stirring occasionally.

This sauce will keep for several weeks in an airtight jar in the refrigerator.

■ **How to Use It:** Mustard-based sauces hail from pork country—so pork is what I'd use this on first. Try it as a finishing sauce for pork shoulder, painted on about 30 minutes before the end of the cooking time. Or try it on a pulled pork sandwich.

Carolina-Style Barbecue Sauce

The recipe that this one is based on won second place in the Mild Mustard Category in the 1994 American Royal International Barbecue Sauce Contest, which is held every year for commercial sauces around the world.

Makes about 3 1/2 cups

½	cup brown sugar, packed
2	teaspoons granulated garlic

2 teaspoons salt
1 teaspoon black pepper
1 teaspoon crushed red pepper
½ teaspoon white pepper
¼ teaspoon cayenne
⅓ cup fresh lemon juice
¼ cup white vinegar
¼ cup apple cider
1 tablespoon Worcestershire sauce
¼ cup molasses
2 cups prepared yellow mustard

Combine all of the dry ingredients in a large nonreactive bowl. Add the lemon juice, vinegar, apple cider, and Worcestershire sauce. Blend with a wire whisk until the spices are dissolved. Then blend in the molasses and mustard.

This sauce will keep for several weeks in an airtight jar in the refrigerator.

■ **How to Use It:** Use this as a finishing sauce for pork shoulder, painted on about 30 minutes before the end of the cooking time. Or try it—warm or chilled—on a pulled pork sandwich.

One Variety of
Piedmont Barbecue Sauce

This is a basic sauce of the Piedmont region of the Carolinas and Georgia. Piedmont is the gently rolling hill country between the Appalachian Mountains and the Atlantic coast.

Makes about 6 cups

4 cups prepared yellow mustard
1 cup fresh lemon juice
1 cup clover honey
½ cup white vinegar
1 teaspoon salt
1 teaspoon cayenne

Combine all of the ingredients in a nonreactive saucepan, and blend well. Bring the mixture to a boil, then reduce the heat and simmer for 10 to 15 minutes, stirring occasionally.

This sauce will keep for several weeks in an airtight jar in the refrigerator.

■ **How to Use It:** Try this simple sauce as a finishing sauce for pork shoulder, painted on about 30 minutes before the end of the cooking time. Mustard fans might enjoy it on a pulled pork sandwich.

Lexington-Style Piedmont Barbecue Sauce

Most barbecue experts talk about Piedmont sauces always being mustard-based, as in the previous recipe. I have no problem with this, but I do remember reading (yes, I must confess that I do read cookbooks) in Jeanne Voltz's cookbook, *Barbecued Ribs, Smoked Butts and Other Great Feeds,* a recipe for a Piedmont (Lexington-style) barbecue sauce that was vinegar-and-ketchup-based. Here's my version. This is a fun, easy barbecue sauce. It's not too hot, but it is a little vinegary.

Makes about 2 cups

1½ cups cider vinegar
1   cup ketchup (store-bought or homemade, pages 238–40)
¼ cup sugar
1   teaspoon salt
½ teaspoon crushed red pepper
¼ teaspoon cayenne

Combine all of the ingredients in a large nonreactive saucepan, and blend well. Bring the mixture to a boil, then reduce the heat, and simmer for 20 to 30 minutes, stirring occasionally.

This sauce will keep for several weeks in an airtight jar in the refrigerator.

■ **How to Use It:** This sauce is great on a pig sandwich—pulled pork on a bun or on bread, topped with cole slaw—the signature dish of Carolina barbecue.

Eastern Carolina
Vinegar Barbecue Sauce

Eastern Carolina—from Raleigh to the coast—is where you'll find vinegar-based sauce. As you can see, it's a pretty simple style of sauce. This particular one has quite a bit of heat to it.

Makes about 2 1/4 cups

- 2 cups cider vinegar
- 1/4 cup brown sugar, packed
- 2 tablespoons sea salt
- 1 tablespoon crushed red pepper
- 1 teaspoon cayenne

Combine all of the ingredients in a nonreactive bowl, and blend well. For the best results, let the sauce stand overnight to allow the flavors to blend.

> If you want a spicier barbecue sauce, add 1 teaspoon of crushed red pepper to a bottle of your favorite sauce.

This sauce will keep for several weeks in an airtight jar in the refrigerator.

■ **How to Use It:** This sauce is another that is great on pulled pork. It's also a good baste and mop. Use warm or chilled.

Oklahoma Vinegar Barbecue Sauce

If you like a thin barbecue sauce, you will like this one. It's a good all-purpose sauce, being fairly tart and not too hot.

Makes about 3 1/2 cups

    2 cups ketchup (store-bought or homemade, pages 238–40)
    2 cups white vinegar
    2 tablespoons Worcestershire sauce
    1 teaspoon black pepper
    1 teaspoon white pepper
    1 teaspoon salt
    2 bay leaves
    ½ teaspoon ground cloves
    ½ teaspoon cayenne

Combine all of the ingredients in a nonreactive saucepan, and blend well. Bring the mixture to a boil, reduce the heat, and simmer for 30 to 40 minutes. Discard the bay leaves.

This sauce will keep for several weeks in an airtight jar in the refrigerator.

■ **How to Use It:** You can use this sauce as a mop or baste, finishing sauce, or dipping sauce.

Sweet and Sour Barbecue Sauce

Several years ago, I spent about six months in Hawaii, teaching at Waianae Elementary School. I also used my time there to pursue some non-barbecue cooking interests. I took, and helped teach, some courses on Chinese cooking. This recipe combines prominent flavors from Chinese and Hawaiian cooking. The pineapple juice and soy sauce give it a distinctive flavorprint.

Makes about 4 cups

    2 cups ketchup (store-bought or homemade, pages 238–40)
    1 cup white vinegar
    1 cup dark brown sugar, packed
    ½ cup pineapple juice
    2 tablespoons soy sauce

1 teaspoon ground ginger
1 teaspoon salt
½ teaspoon cayenne

Combine all of the ingredients in a nonreactive saucepan, and blend well. Bring the mixture to a boil, then reduce the heat and simmer for 15 to 20 minutes, stirring occasionally.

This sauce will keep for up to 2 weeks in an airtight jar in the refrigerator.

■ **How to Use It:** This is a good dipping sauce for chicken, ribs, and shrimp.

■ **Variation:** You can give this a Caribbean flavorprint by substituting 1 teaspoon allspice for the ground ginger, and adding ½ teaspoon of ground dried habanero.

Tangerine Barbecue Sauce

This recipe has a very interesting background. It was developed for the Hyatt Regency Hotel on Cheju Island, South Korea, with the help of Soo Chun Lee, executive sous chef. Cheju Island is several hundred miles off the coast of South Korea. It is a garden island with nude beaches, but it was my luck to be there out of season. In the off-season the attraction is not the beaches but the casinos, one of which has a restaurant where you can order a $15,000 meal for one—now that's high rolling!

I was in South Korea on a trade mission to teach and promote Midwestern barbecue and barbecue products. The Cheju Hyatt did a three-month barbecue promotion, using this sauce recipe for the big barbecue shindig. The recipe was developed for the specific purpose of utilizing tangerines and tangerine juice, for which Cheju Island is famous. The tangerine is a symbol of good luck and prosperity in Asia.

Makes about 8 cups

1 cup brown sugar, packed
3 tablespoons chili powder
2 tablespoons black pepper
1 tablespoon ground ginger
1 tablespoon dry mustard powder

1   tablespoon onion salt
1   tablespoon granulated garlic
1   tablespoon sea salt
1   teaspoon ground coriander
1   teaspoon cayenne
1   teaspoon crushed red pepper
¼   teaspoon powdered bay leaf
1   quart tangerine juice with pulp
¾   cup cider vinegar
¼   cup clover honey
¼   cup Worcestershire sauce
1   12-ounce can tomato paste
1   cup ketchup (store-bought or homemade, pages 238–40)

Combine the brown sugar, chili powder, black pepper, ginger, mustard, onion salt, garlic, sea salt, coriander, cayenne, red pepper, and bay leaf in a saucepan. Blend in the tangerine juice, vinegar, honey, and Worcestershire sauce with a wire whisk.

Heat the mixture over medium heat. Blend in the tomato paste and ketchup. Bring the mixture to a boil, reduce the heat, and simmer for 30 minutes, stirring occasionally.

This sauce will keep for 1 to 2 weeks in an airtight jar in the refrigerator.

■ **How to Use It:** This sauce is good as a finishing sauce or dipping sauce with any kind of poultry or pork. In Korea, it was a favorite on duck.

■ **Variation:** You can substitute fresh orange juice for the tangerine juice; even better would be to substitute bottled mango juice.

Honey Teriyaki Barbecue Sauce

The Japanese don't barbecue, but they do grill—after painting the meat with a sweet soy mixture. This sauce conjures up those flavors. You can use it as a dipping sauce for any grilled meat, poultry, or fish in conjunction with a teriyaki marinade in chapter 3. Or skip the marinade, and just use the sauce to glaze the meat on the grill or to dip into at the table.

Makes about 3 cups

½ cup light brown sugar, packed
1 teaspoon ground ginger
1 teaspoon granulated garlic
2 cups pineapple juice
1 cup soy sauce
½ cup clover honey
2 tablespoons arrowroot*
3 tablespoons cold water

Combine the sugar, ginger, and garlic in a medium-size nonreactive saucepan. With a wire whisk, blend in the pineapple juice and soy sauce. Stir in the honey. Bring the mixture to a boil over medium-high heat. Make a paste with the arrowroot and cold water. When the pineapple mixture comes to a boil, slowly add the arrowroot mixture and blend well with the wire whisk. Bring to a boil again, reduce the heat, and simmer for about 2 minutes or until a sheen comes to the sauce.

This sauce will keep for about 1 week in an airtight jar in the refrigerator.

■ **How to Use It:** This can be used as a finishing sauce, as a warm or chilled dipping sauce, and as a stir-frying sauce. It goes particularly well with chicken. I get hungry just thinking about it.

*****Note:** If you don't stock arrowroot, which is used as a thickener, you can substitute 4½ teaspoons cornstarch, but you will need to boil the sauce for an extra 2 minutes.

Smoky Peach Barbecue Sauce

Anything goes in barbecue these days, and this sauce proves it. Peach and peach schnapps give this sauce a strong fruity presence.

Makes about 2 cups

1   16-ounce can sliced peaches, drained and
    their liquid reserved
1   cup ketchup (store-bought or homemade, pages 238–40)
¼   cup brown sugar, packed
3   tablespoons fresh lemon juice
1   tablespoon peach schnapps (optional)
1   teaspoon liquid smoke
1   teaspoon ground ginger
1   teaspoon salt
1   teaspoon grated lemon zest
½   teaspoon ground cinnamon
¼   teaspoon ground allspice

Purée the peaches in a food processor fitted with a steel blade or in a blender. Combine the rest of the ingredients, including the peach liquid, in a nonreactive saucepan. Blend in the puréed peaches. Bring the mixture to a boil, reduce the heat, and simmer for 15 to 20 minutes, stirring occasionally.

This sauce will keep for up to 2 weeks in an airtight jar in the refrigerator.

■ **How to Use It:** This is a great chicken and rib finishing barbecue sauce. It's also good served cold as a dip with potato chips.

■ **Variation:** Substitute 2 fresh mangoes, peeled, pitted, and diced, for the peaches.

Cranberry Pineapple Barbecue Sauce

Thanksgiving may never be the same. Contemplate bringing a juicy barbecued bird to the table, and replacing the traditional cranberry sauce with this tangy sweet-and-sour barbecue sauce.

Makes about 4 cups

- 2   tablespoons vegetable oil
- ½   cup minced onions
- 1   garlic clove, pressed
- 1   16-ounce can cranberry sauce with whole cranberries
- 1   8-ounce can crushed pineapple with juice
- 1   cup ketchup (store-bought or homemade, pages 238–40)
- 1   cup brown sugar, packed
- ¼   cup soy sauce
- ¼   cup white vinegar
- 1   teaspoon ground ginger
- 1   teaspoon white pepper
- 1   teaspoon salt

Heat the oil in a nonreactive saucepan over medium heat. Add the onions and garlic and sauté until transparent, but not brown, about 4 minutes. Add the cranberry sauce, pineapple, ketchup, sugar, soy sauce, vinegar, ginger, pepper, and salt. Blend in well, and simmer the mixture, stirring occasionally, for 30 to 40 minutes. Let the sauce cool.

This sauce will keep for up to 2 weeks in an airtight jar in the refrigerator.

■ How to Use It: Use this barbecue sauce with any kind of poultry or pork—warm or cold.

Raspberry Barbecue Sauce

Raspberries are a popular ingredient these days. You find them in vinegars, salad dressings, marinades, and now, barbecue sauce. In this sauce, the raspberries don't leap out at you directly—they just hang back and nod. See if you can recognize them.

Makes about 4 cups

1   10-ounce package frozen raspberries in syrup, thawed
3   tablespoons fresh lemon juice
½   teaspoon salt
1½ cups sugar
2   cups ketchup (store-bought or homemade, pages 238–40)
¼   cup brown sugar
¼   cup white vinegar
2   tablespoons chili powder
2   teaspoons black pepper
1   teaspoon salt
1   teaspoon ground allspice
½   teaspoon ground ginger
¼   teaspoon ground cloves

Place the raspberries, lemon juice, and salt in a food processor fitted with a steel blade or in a blender, and process until smooth. Strain to remove the raspberry seeds. Pour the mixture into a nonreactive saucepan, and stir in the sugar. Cook over medium heat, stirring, until the sugar has dissolved. Simmer for 30 minutes, stirring occasionally. Add the rest of the ingredients to the raspberry mixture, blending well. Simmer for another 20 to 30 minutes, continuing to stir occasionally. Be careful to avoid scorching the sauce at the bottom of the pan.

This sauce will keep for up to 2 weeks in an airtight jar in the refrigerator.

■ **How to Use It:** This barbecue sauce goes with brisket, pork, chicken—you name it. It goes with any kind of barbecue. It's got a lot of sugar in it, so it works best as a dipping sauce, warm or chilled.

Purple Plum Barbecue Sauce

You've got to love a sauce like this. It tastes great, and will have all your guests scratching their heads trying to figure out just what is in it. The flavor is so rich and complex, I dare anyone to taste it and guess the recipe.

Makes about 3 1/2 cups

- 1 16-ounce can purple plums with syrup
- 1 tablespoon vegetable oil
- 1/2 cup lemonade concentrate, thawed
- 1/2 cup chili sauce
- 1/4 cup soy sauce
- 1/4 cup minced onion
- 1 tablespoon prepared yellow mustard
- 2 teaspoons Worcestershire sauce
- 1 teaspoon ground ginger
- 1 teaspoon salt

Drain the plums and reserve the syrup. Remove and discard the pits. Combine the plums and reserved syrup in a blender or a food processor fitted with a steel blade, and blend until smooth.

In a nonreactive saucepan, heat the oil over medium heat. Add the onion, and sauté until soft but not brown, about 3 minutes. Add the rest of the ingredients, including the puréed plums, and bring to a boil. Reduce the heat and simmer for 15 to 20 minutes, stirring occasionally.

This sauce will keep for up to 2 weeks in an airtight jar in the refrigerator.

■ **How to Use It:** This sauce is at its best on poultry. It is truly great with smoked duck. Serve it warm or cold as a dipping sauce.

Berry Berry Barbecue Sauce

Here's a sauce to try when you are looking for some new flavor to spark the perfectly good sauce you already have in a jar in the refrigerator. Nobody will guess the ingredients in this one, either.

Makes about 4 1/2 cups

2   cups tomato-based barbecue sauce
1   cup strawberry preserves
1   cup jellied cranberry sauce
¼   cup water
¼   cup brown sugar, packed
2   tablespoons soy sauce
2   tablespoons chili powder
½   teaspoon garlic powder
¼   teaspoon ground allspice
¼   teaspoon ground cloves

Combine all of the ingredients in a nonreactive saucepan, and bring to a boil. Stir until the jellies melt and blend in well. Reduce the heat, and simmer for 30 minutes, stirring occasionally. Be careful to avoid scorching the sauce at the bottom of the pan.

Use this sauce warm or chilled. It will keep for several weeks in an airtight jar in the refrigerator.

■ How to Use It: Besides being a good dipping sauce, this sauce is great for glazing. It makes very nontraditional barbecue, but it's great on pork, ribs, and chicken. Brush it on about 30 minutes before the end of the cooking time.

Orange Barbecue Sauce

This sauce brings out the best in poultry.

Makes about 2 cups

- 1 cup orange juice
- ½ cup water
- ½ cup white wine vinegar
- ⅓ cup sugar
- ¼ cup clover honey
- 1 teaspoon chili powder
- 1 teaspoon crushed dried rosemary leaves
- 1 teaspoon salt
- ½ teaspoon white pepper

Combine all of the ingredients in a nonreactive saucepan. Bring the mixture to a boil, reduce the heat, and simmer for 15 minutes, stirring occasionally. Be careful to avoid scorching the sauce at the bottom of the pan.

This sauce will keep for up to 2 weeks in an airtight jar in the refrigerator.

■ **How to Use It:** Serve this cooled, as a dipping sauce with chicken, duck, and quail.

West Indies Guava Barbecue Sauce

This recipe uses guava for its fruity base, an exotic tropical fruit related to cloves and allspice. It has a distinctive spicy, sweet-tart flavor, which makes it very interesting in a barbecue sauce. You may ask, how the heck am I going to get a quart of guava pulp in the U.S.? If you live in California, Florida, or Hawaii, you may be able to find fresh guavas. Buy them ripe, peel them, purée them in a blender, then strain. Elsewhere, look for canned whole guavas or canned paste in Latin markets.

Makes about 4 cups

1	3-inch cinnamon stick
1	teaspoon whole cloves
1	teaspoon celery seeds
1	teaspoon black peppercorns
1	dried chile pepper
1	bay leaf
1	quart strained guava pulp
1	tablespoon dry mustard powder
2	teaspoons sea salt
1	cup sugar
1	cup white vinegar

In a small cheesecloth bag, combine the cinnamon stick, cloves, celery seeds, peppercorns, chile pepper, and bay leaf, and tie to secure well. Lightly pound the spices to release more of their flavor.

In a heavy-bottomed saucepan, combine the guava pulp, mustard, and sea salt. Add the spice bag, sugar, and vinegar, and simmer over medium heat until thick, stirring often to prevent scorching.

This sauce will keep for 1 week in an airtight jar in the refrigerator.

■ **How to Use It:** Serve this sauce warm or at room temperature as a dipping sauce. It makes an excellent glaze for smoked turkey and barbecued chicken. It can also double as a salad dressing for avocados. Or, use it as a salad dressing base and whisk in a little oil.

■ **Variations:** You can change the flavor of the sauce with some changes in the spices. I like to add some fresh gingerroot and/or whole allspice berries to the spice bag.

Spicy Peanut Sauce

In Indonesia, they grill small cubes of meat, poultry, and fish on skewers and serve it with a spicy peanut sauce like this one. The dish is called satay.

Makes about 3 cups

¼ cup (½ stick) unsalted butter
1 cup minced onions
1 bay leaf
2 cups chunky peanut butter
2 cups chicken stock or water
2 tablespoons brown sugar
2 tablespoons fresh lemon juice
1 teaspoon salt
½ teaspoon cayenne

In a medium-size nonreactive saucepan, melt the butter over medium heat. Add the onions and bay leaf, and sauté until the onions are soft, about 4 minutes. Add the peanut butter, stock, sugar, lemon juice, salt, and cayenne. Blend well. Simmer the mixture for 10 to 15 minutes, stirring frequently to prevent the sauce from sticking to the bottom of the pan. Remove the bay leaf and discard it.

This sauce will keep for several weeks in an airtight jar in the refrigerator if made with water. If made with stock, it will keep for up to 1 week.

■ **How to Use It:** This is a very good sauce for grilled shrimp, scallops, or any fish. It's also good with chicken and pork. You can even use it as a dip for vegetables. Serve it warm or at room temperature.

■ **Variations:** Substitute peanut oil or any vegetable oil for the butter. Substitute 2 to 3 teaspoons soy sauce for the salt. Instead of the cayenne, add a few tablespoons of finely chopped hot chile pepper.

Cashew Lemon Sauce

Cashew butter, or as I call it, cashew peanut butter, forms the basis of this sauce. It can be purchased at health food stores. In a pinch, you could substitute peanut butter and peanuts, but the flavor won't be the same.

Makes about 1 3/4 cups

- 1   cup cashew butter
- ¼   cup finely chopped roasted unsalted cashew nuts
- 3   tablespoons fresh lemon juice
- 2   tablespoons chicken stock or water
- 2   tablespoons clover honey
- 1   tablespoon grated lemon zest
- 1   teaspoon curry powder
- 1   teaspoon sea salt
- ½   teaspoon dry mustard powder
- ½   teaspoon black pepper

Combine all of the ingredients in a nonreactive saucepan, and blend well. Simmer for 10 to 15 minutes over medium heat, stirring constantly.

Use the sauce warm or at room temperature. This sauce will keep for several weeks in an airtight jar in the refrigerator if made with water. If made with chicken stock, it will keep for up to 1 week.

■ How to Use It: This sauce, like most nut sauces, is good on fish, grilled shrimp, and pork.

Nutty Bacon Barbecue Sauce

I know the combination of nuts and bacon may sound odd in a barbecue sauce, but don't laugh until you've tried it.

Makes about 8 1/2 cups

SEASONING MIX:

2 teaspoons black pepper
1 teaspoon sea salt
1 teaspoon onion powder
1 teaspoon garlic powder
½ teaspoon white pepper
½ teaspoon cayenne

SAUCE:

½ pound bacon, minced
1½ cups diced onions
2 cups beef bouillon or broth
2 cups chili sauce
1 cup clover honey
½ cup pecans, toasted and chopped
⅓ cup orange juice
¼ cup fresh lemon juice
1 tablespoon minced orange zest
1 tablespoon minced lemon zest
1 teaspoon crushed red pepper
¼ cup (½ stick) butter, cut into small pieces and kept cold

Combine the ingredients for the seasoning mix, and set aside.

Fry the bacon in a large nonreactive saucepan over high heat, until it is crispy. Stir in the onions, cover the pan, and continue cooking, stirring occasionally, until onions are dark brown, but not burned, about 8 or 9 minutes. Stir in the seasoning mixture, and cook for one more minute. Add the rest of the ingredients, except the butter. Bring the mixture to a boil. Reduce the heat and simmer for 30 minutes, stirring frequently. Add the butter, and blend it in with a wire whisk until it is melted and incorporated into the sauce.

Let the mixture cool for about 30 minutes. Pour it into a blender or a food processor fitted with a steel blade, and purée until the bacon and pecans are finely chopped.

This sauce will keep for up to 1 week in an airtight jar in the refrigerator.

■ How to Use It: Serve this warm—it's a great dipping sauce for poultry and pork. I also like this sauce cooked longer, until it is reduced by a half, and used as a party dip with chips.

White Barbecue Sauce

If you thought tartar sauce was the best accompaniment for grilled or fried fish, try this. You may never dip into tartar sauce again.

Makes about 3 cups

1 cup mayonnaise
1 cup salad dressing (such as Miracle Whip)
½ cup white wine vinegar
¼ cup fresh lemon juice
¼ cup water
2 tablespoons white Worcestershire sauce
2 tablespoons sugar
1 tablespoon fresh-ground black pepper
1 tablespoon fresh-ground white pepper
1 teaspoon dry mustard powder
1 teaspoon salt
½ teaspoon ground ginger
½ teaspoon ground allspice

Combine all of the ingredients in a large nonreactive bowl. Blend well with a wire whisk.

Keep this sauce refrigerated when not in use. It will keep for up to 2 weeks in an airtight jar in the refrigerator.

■ **How to Use It:** Serve this sauce with grilled fish.

6

Salsas, Relishes, and Ketchups

This is my what-else chapter, as in, What else do you need for great-tasting barbecue? You need homemade ketchups, relishes, and salsas to go on the table next to the meat. The flavor of these condiments is the perfect match for the smoke-flavored meats.

Barbecue is about tradition, but it is also about breaking the rules. The barbecue arena has expanded by leaps and bounds because chefs are willing to experiment with flavors. For example, many barbecuers are now using fruits, such as peaches, cranberries, blackberries, raspberries, and apricots, to name a few, in their sauces. The number of different ingredients that can be combined in new and different ways is endless. When it comes to barbecuing, a little innovation and imagination can bring great rewards.

■ Salsas and Relishes ■

What does salsa have to do with barbecue? A lot. Salsa is always a great barbecue accompaniment, and today it is on the cutting edge of barbecue. Barbecuers are experimenting with salsa more than anything else, inventing new and exciting recipes as they go along. I think salsa is the future of barbecue, and the future is looking bright.

In the case of *salsa,* I think the standard dictionary definition falls short:

salsa *n. Chiefly Southwestern U.S.* A spicy sauce made of tomatoes, onions, and chili peppers, eaten with tortilla chips or other Mexican food.

This definition is much too limiting. My definition of salsa is "A balanced combination of compatible ingredients and spices." The kicker in this definition is that you decide what is compatible and what isn't, so any combination of ingredients goes! The important thing to strive for in creating your own salsa is balance between the ingredients. Salsas are usually composed of a flavorful but relatively unobtrusive-tasting base, such as tomatoes, tomatillos, apples, peaches, or grapes, and a smaller proportion of zesty ingredients, such as lime juice, onions, hot peppers, cilantro, and garlic. The variations are endless, but a rough guideline to follow is ⅔ of the base ingredient to ⅓ combined zesty ingredients.

A more traditional condiment for barbecue, but one closely related to salsa, is relish. The dictionary definition of relish is as follows:

relish *n.* **1.** A spicy or savory condiment or appetizer, such as chutney or olives. **2.** A condiment of chopped sweet pickle.

Folks used to pickle a lot of the vegetables from their gardens every summer. Some of them got chopped and blended into mixtures like corn relish and piccalilli. A lot of what used to be called a relish now gets called a salsa, which is why I've grouped them together in this chapter.

Salsa Cruda

Salsa Cruda, which means uncooked salsa, is best served fresh. Keep it chilled until you are ready to serve it.

Makes about 3 1/2 cups

- 2 cups peeled, seeded, and chopped ripe tomatoes
- 1 cup minced onions
- ¼ cup fresh lime juice
- 2 tablespoons minced fresh cilantro
- 2 tablespoons fresh or canned minced small green chiles, such as serranos (seeding is optional)
- 2 garlic cloves, pressed
- 2 teaspoons chili powder
- 1 teaspoon black pepper
- 1 teaspoon salt

Combine all of the ingredients in a nonreactive bowl, and toss gently. Refrigerate for several hours to let the flavors combine. Adjust the seasonings, if needed, before serving.

Fresh salsa will last for 2 to 3 days in the refrigerator, but it is generally best on the day it is made.

■ **How to Use It:** This is one of my favorites to go with barbecued or smoked pork. Of course, you can use it as a dip with chips, on top of nachos or tacos, or in any other way you usually use salsa.

■ **Variation:** For a milder version, replace the 1 cup minced onions with ½ cup minced red onions and ¼ cup minced green onions. Reduce the chiles to 1 tablespoon, and omit the garlic and the chili powder. Add salt and pepper to taste.

Citrus Salsa Cruda

This is a traditional salsa with a citrusy tang.

Makes about 3 1/2 cups

2   cups peeled, seeded, and diced ripe tomatoes
1   cup diced white onions
½   cup minced fresh cilantro
¼   cup minced fresh parsley
¼   cup orange juice
¼   cup vegetable oil
3   tablespoons fresh lime juice
3   garlic cloves, pressed
1   jalapeño, seeded and minced
1   teaspoon black pepper
1   teaspoon salt

Combine all of the ingredients in a nonreactive bowl, and toss gently. Refrigerate for several hours to let the flavors combine. Adjust the seasonings, if needed, before serving.

Fresh salsa will last for 2 to 3 days in the refrigerator, but it is generally best on the day it is made.

■ **How to Use It:** Serve with grilled orange roughy or grilled cod. This salsa takes well to most white-fleshed fish. It's also a natural with shellfish, especially grilled shrimp and scallops.

■ **Variation:** For extra citrus flavor, you can add half a grapefruit, finely chopped.

> **CAUTION:**
> When you are working with spicy peppers, wear rubber or plastic gloves. The volatile oils in the peppers will make your eyes sore and watery. So don't rub them!

Tomatillo-Tomato Salsa

If you haven't made the acquaintance of tomatillos, red tomatoes' little green cousins, you should. When added raw to a salsa, they add the combined flavors of lemon, apple, and herbs. They also provide an acid backbone to a sauce. Usually you buy them with their papery husk intact. The husk is easily removed, but be sure to wash the sticky tomatillos inside.

Makes about 3 cups

1 cup peeled and chopped tomatillos
1 cup peeled and finely chopped ripe tomatoes
½ cup diced Spanish or Bermuda onions
¼ cup minced fresh cilantro
¼ cup fresh lime juice
1 tablespoon minced roasted jalapeño, peeled and seeded*
1 tablespoon minced fresh oregano leaves
1 tablespoon pressed garlic
1 teaspoon black pepper
1 teaspoon sea salt
½ teaspoon ground cumin

Combine all of the ingredients in a nonreactive bowl, toss gently, and mix well. Let the mixture set in the refrigerator for 3 to 4 hours so the flavors will blend.

Fresh salsa will last for 2 to 3 days in the refrigerator, but it is generally best on the day it is made.

■ **How to Use It:** Serve this salsa with grilled fish, steak, or pork tenderloin.

***Note:** To roast a jalapeño, grill it until blackened on all sides, turning every few minutes. Put it in a bag for 10 minutes to loosen the skin. Then peel away the charred skin.

How do you serve salsa with your barbecue? When it was legal in competition, I liked to put a line of this salsa, one inch wide and one inch tall, right down the middle of the slice of pork, chicken, or other meat. You can also serve it to the side.

Tomatillo Salsa

When you get hooked on the flavor of these little lemony fruits, this is the salsa to make.

Makes about 1 1/2 cups

1 cup diced tomatillos
½ cup diced red onions
¼ cup seeded and diced Anaheim chile pepper
1 tablespoon minced fresh cilantro
1 tablespoon minced fresh parsley
1 tablespoon diced red jalapeño
2 tablespoons white vinegar
1 tablespoon vegetable oil
1 teaspoon black pepper
1 teaspoon salt

Combine all of the ingredients in a nonreactive bowl, and mix well. Let the mixture rest in the refrigerator for at least 2 hours so that the flavors blend.

Fresh salsa will last for 2 to 3 days in the refrigerator, but it is generally best on the day it is made.

■ **How to Use It:** This is a delightful, peppery topping for steak or fish.

■ **Variations:** If you can't find a red (fully ripened) jalapeño, substitute a green one.

Salsa Verde

Salsa Verde means green salsa. The color comes from the tomatillos, chiles, and cilantro.

Makes about 2 1/4 cups

1½ cups chopped tomatillos
3   tablespoons chopped white onion
2   tablespoons minced green onion, green and white parts
2   tablespoons seeded and diced serrano chile
2   tablespoons minced fresh cilantro
2   tablespoons minced fresh parsley
4   garlic cloves, pressed
1   teaspoon salt
1   teaspoon black pepper
2   tablespoons white vinegar
2   tablespoons cold water

Place the tomatillos, onions, serrano, cilantro, parsley, garlic, salt, pepper, and vinegar in a blender or in a food processor fitted with a steel blade. Blend to a purée, adding the water a little at a time. Taste, and adjust seasonings. Let the mixture stand for at least 1 hour to allow the flavors to blend.

Fresh salsa will last for 2 to 3 days in the refrigerator, but it is generally best on the day it is made.

■ **How to Use It:** Serve this with grilled fish or chicken.

Zesty Jícama Salsa

Jícama, a.k.a. the Mexican potato, is sweet and nutty in flavor and adds a lot of crunchy texture to a salsa. It is a round, bulbous root vegetable with a light brown skin and white flesh. You can find jícamas in most supermarkets from November through May.

Makes about 3 1/2 cups

2   cups seeded and chopped ripe plum tomatoes
1   cup peeled and diced jícama
1   4-ounce can green chiles, drained and diced
¼   cup tomato juice

2 tablespoons Louisiana-style hot sauce
2 tablespoons minced green onion, green and white parts
2 tablespoons minced fresh cilantro
2 garlic cloves, pressed
Salt to taste

Combine all of the ingredients in a nonreactive bowl, and mix well. Let the mixture rest in the refrigerator for at least 2 hours to blend the flavors.

Fresh salsa will last for 2 to 3 days in the refrigerator, but it is generally best on the day it is made.

■ How to Use It: This salsa is good on grilled eggplant, on fish, or on a good medium-rare fillet of beef.

Savory Salsa

The flavor combination is more Mediterranean than Mexican, but this is the best fish salsa that my barbecue team and I have, and it's not too bad on beef, either.

Makes about 3 cups

1 pound ripe plum tomatoes, seeded and chopped
½ cup minced fennel bulb
½ cup diced white onions
½ cup diced celery
¼ cup minced fresh basil
3 tablespoons extra-virgin olive oil
3 tablespoons balsamic vinegar
2 tablespoons Dijon-style mustard
2 garlic cloves, pressed
½ teaspoon salt
½ teaspoon white pepper

Combine all of the ingredients in a nonreactive bowl, and toss to mix. Refrigerate for several hours to let the flavors combine. Adjust the seasonings, if needed, before serving.

Fresh salsa will last for 2 to 3 days in the refrigerator, but it is generally best on the day it is made.

■ How to Use It: You can serve this salsa with fish, chicken, or beef.

Apple Lemongrass Salsa

Lemongrass is one of the most important flavors in Thai cooking, so naturally if you can't find it in your supermarket, look for it wherever Thai foods are sold. When you buy lemongrass fresh, it looks like a scallion with tougher, gray-green leaves. Use just the bottom 4 inches of the stem. The lemongrass gives a very lemony perfume to the relish.

Makes about 3 cups

1   pound Granny Smith apples, peeled, cored, and diced
1   cup diced Spanish onions
2   limes, peeled so no white pith remains, and diced
2   tablespoons fresh lime juice
2   stalks lemongrass, chopped (bottom 4 inches only)
¼   cup minced fresh cilantro
2   teaspoons sugar
1   teaspoon salt

Combine all of the ingredients in a large nonreactive bowl, and blend well. Cover, and let sit in the refrigerator for several hours before serving. This is best on the day it is made.

■ **How to Use It:** This relish is good served on grilled chicken breasts, lamb chops, fish, or shrimp.

Apple Salsa

Tomatoes are a traditional salsa base, and apple-based salsas are becoming more popular all the time. In this salsa, apples and tomatoes together form the base.

Makes about 5 cups

2   cups peeled, cored, and diced apples
2   cups peeled, seeded, and chopped ripe tomatoes
½   cup diced onions
½   cup minced celery
¼   cup diced red bell pepper
2   tablespoons sugar
1   tablespoon finely minced fresh mint
1   tablespoon grated fresh horseradish

1   clove garlic, pressed
1   teaspoon salt
½   teaspoon black pepper

Combine all of the ingredients in a nonreactive saucepan, and bring to a boil. Reduce the heat, and simmer for 5 to 7 minutes.
    This salsa will keep for 3 to 4 days in the refrigerator.

■ **How to Use It:** Serve this salsa hot or cold with pork shoulder or tenderloin.

Apple and Mint Relish

You can heat the jam before mixing to make it easier to incorporate.

Makes about 2 cups

1   pound Granny Smith apples, peeled
¼   cup apricot jam
2   tablespoons fresh lemon juice
2   tablespoons minced fresh spearmint
1   teaspoon peeled, grated, and minced fresh gingerroot
½   teaspoon salt
¼   teaspoon white pepper

Grate the apple, and combine immediately with the remaining ingredients in a nonreactive mixing bowl. Mix well. Taste, and adjust the seasoning. Let the mixture sit for about 30 minutes to allow the flavors to blend. This relish is best served on the day it is made.

■ **How to Use It:** This relish works very well with lamb, beef, or grilled fish.

Barbecue Salsa

What do you call a cross between a barbecue sauce and a salsa? Barbecue salsa, of course. The recipe requires a cup of tomato-based barbecue sauce or ketchup. Feel free to use any homemade stuff that you happen to have on hand.

Makes about 5 cups

- 2 cups chopped red ripe tomatoes
- 1 cup seeded and diced cucumber (peeled if waxed)
- ½ cup diced red bell pepper
- ½ cup diced green bell pepper
- ½ cup diced yellow bell pepper
- ½ cup minced red onions
- ½ cup white vinegar
- ⅓ cup clover honey
- 2 teaspoons chili powder
- 1 teaspoon black pepper
- 1 teaspoon salt
- ½ teaspoon dry mustard powder
- ½ teaspoon celery seeds
- ½ teaspoon ground cinnamon
- ¼ teaspoon ground allspice
- ¼ teaspoon cayenne
- 1 cup tomato-based barbecue sauce or ketchup

Combine all of the ingredients, except the barbecue sauce, in a nonreactive saucepan with a tight-fitting lid. Place over low heat, and cook the mixture for about 10 to 15 minutes or until the vegetables have softened. Blend in the barbecue sauce, and simmer for another 10 minutes. Taste, and adjust the seasonings. Cool to room temperature.

Use this salsa chilled or at room temperature. It will keep for several days in the refrigerator.

■ **How to Use It:** I like to use this salsa in competition on my barbecued chicken and pork shoulder—it's a real winner! It's also excellent on grilled pork sausage topped with a little bit of sharp cheddar cheese.

Pineapple Jalapeño Salsa

This is a nice, light, peppery salsa.

Makes about 3 cups

2   cups chopped fresh sweet pineapple
½   cup diced tomatillos
¼   cup diced red bell pepper
1   tablespoon fresh lime juice
1   tablespoon rice wine vinegar
1   tablespoon vegetable oil
1   tablespoon grated fresh gingerroot
2   teaspoons seeded and minced jalapeño
2   teaspoons minced fresh mint
1   teaspoon sea salt

Combine all of the ingredients in a bowl, and mix well. Cover, and let sit several hours in the refrigerator. Taste, and adjust seasonings before serving.

Fresh salsa will last for 2 to 3 days in the refrigerator, but it is generally best on the day it is made.

One thing to remember about salsas is that besides being good on barbecue, they are also tasty on chips and grilled vegetables.

■ **How to Use It:** This recipe will go with any barbecued or grilled meat, fish, or shrimp.

■ **Variation:** Substitute 1 16-ounce can of crushed pineapple for the fresh pineapple. Drain well, and save the juice for another use, such as one of the teriyaki or Hawaiian marinades in chapter 3.

Pineapple Salsa

This salsa is light and delicious with a kiss of heat.

Makes about 3 cups

- 2 cups finely chopped fresh pineapple
- ½ cup diced red bell pepper
- ¼ cup minced green onions, green and white parts
- ¼ cup fresh lime juice
- ¼ cup white wine vinegar
- 2 tablespoons minced fresh parsley
- 2 tablespoons minced fresh cilantro
- 1 tablespoon seeded and minced jalapeño
- 2 garlic cloves, pressed
- 1 teaspoon sea salt

Combine all of the ingredients in a bowl. Toss lightly to mix. Cover, and refrigerate for several hours. Taste, and adjust seasonings before serving.

Fresh salsa will last for 2 to 3 days in the refrigerator, but it is generally best on the day it is made.

■ **How to Use It:** Serve this salsa with pork, chicken, or fish.

■ **Variation:** Substitute 1 16-ounce can of crushed pineapple for the fresh pineapple. Drain well, and save the juice for another use, such as one of the teriyaki or Hawaiian marinades in chapter 3.

Barbecue Peach Salsa

Peaches and smoked meat are a great barbecue match.

Makes about 3 1/2 cups

- 2 cups peeled and coarsely chopped ripe peaches
- 1 cup peeled, seeded, and coarsely chopped ripe plum tomatoes
- ¼ cup sugar
- ¼ cup clover honey
- ¼ cup white vinegar
- 1 tablespoon seeded and minced jalapeño

2 teaspoons chili powder
2 garlic cloves, pressed
1 teaspoon salt
½ teaspoon white pepper

Combine all of the ingredients in a bowl, cover, and let sit in the refrigerator for several hours, or even better, overnight. Adjust the seasoning, if necessary, before serving.

Serve chilled or at room temperature. This will keep for 3 to 4 days in the refrigerator.

■ **How to Use It:** This salsa is great on burgers, beef, pork, hot dogs, and grilled fish.

All-Purpose Salsa

This salsa recipe requires cooking. The reason to make a cooked salsa is that it keeps without losing flavor. The reason to avoid a cooked salsa, of course, is that it lacks that lively freshness.

Makes about 2 1/2 cups

2 tablespoons olive oil
½ cup minced Spanish or Bermuda onions
2 garlic cloves, minced or pressed
2 cups peeled, seeded, and chopped ripe tomatoes
1 4-ounce can green chiles, rinsed and diced
1 teaspoon black pepper
1 teaspoon salt
1 tablespoon minced fresh cilantro

In a nonreactive saucepan, heat the oil over medium-high heat. Add the onions and garlic, and sauté until soft, but not browned, about 4 minutes. Add the tomatoes, chiles, pepper, and salt. Simmer for 15 to 20 minutes. Taste, and adjust the seasoning. Stir in the cilantro. Cool to room temperature before serving.

This salsa will keep for up to 1 week in the refrigerator.

■ **How to Use It:** This is a good all-purpose salsa, great with barbecued pork or beef, handy with grilled meats and fish of all types, and excellent as a dip with chips.

Black-Eyed Pea Salsa

You could call this a relish if you wanted to. It tastes great with any kind of barbecued meat. Black-eyed peas can be found canned, but they don't take as much time to cook as other dried beans, so you may as well boil up your own. Don't presoak them overnight or they will disintegrate. Just simmer them for 45 to 60 minutes or until they are cooked all the way through.

Makes about 4 cups

¼ cup diced bacon
¼ cup diced red onion
2 tablespoons diced shallots
2 garlic cloves, pressed
½ cup olive oil
¼ cup Champagne vinegar
½ teaspoon dried thyme leaves
½ teaspoon crushed red pepper
2 cups cooked black-eyed peas
1 cup finely diced ripe tomatoes
½ cup chopped green onions, white and green parts
2 tablespoons honey mustard
1 teaspoon black pepper
1 teaspoon salt

Fry the bacon over medium heat in a nonreactive saucepan until it is crisp. Remove the bacon, and set it aside. In the grease left in the pan, sauté the red onion, shallots, and garlic until they are tender, about 5 minutes. Add the olive oil, vinegar, thyme, and crushed red pepper. Cook for 3 minutes, then reduce the heat to low, and add the rest of the ingredients. Simmer for 10 to 15 minutes. Taste, and adjust the seasonings.

This salsa will keep for 4 to 5 days in the refrigerator.

■ **How to Use It:** Serve this warm with a meat entrée, either on the side or over the top.

New-Fashioned Corn Relish

Pink peppercorns and two types of fresh sweet corn give this
relish a new and lively twist.

Makes about 4 1/2 cups

2 cups yellow corn kernels (from about 4 ears
of corn), blanched*

1 cup white corn kernels (from about 2 ears
of corn), blanched*

½ cup diced red onions

½ cup diced green bell pepper

½ cup diced red bell pepper

¼ cup cider vinegar

¼ cup clover honey

2 teaspoons pink peppercorns, cracked**

1 teaspoon kosher salt

¼ teaspoon ground turmeric

Combine all of the ingredients in a nonreactive mixing bowl,
and blend well. Taste, and adjust the seasonings. Then cover,
and refrigerate for at least 2 hours before serving.

This tastes best on the day it is made, but it will keep in the
refrigerator for several days.

■ **How to Use It:** This relish is wonderful on smoked sausages,
Polish sausage, or any pork or fish.

***Note:** You can substitute 3 cups frozen and thawed corn for
the fresh corn, but the flavor and sweetness will be diminished.

****Note:** It's the pink peppercorns that make this "new-
fashioned." If you don't have them on hand or can't find any,
substitute white pepper to taste.

Old-Fashioned Corn Relish

If you like corn on the cob, you'll like this relish. Use it right on your sandwich, or on the side.

Makes about 4 cups

1   9-ounce package frozen corn kernels, thawed and drained
½   cup minced red onions
½   cup minced celery
½   cup minced red bell pepper
¼   cup sweet pickle relish
2   tablespoons sugar
2   tablespoons arrowroot or 4½ teaspoons cornstarch
3   tablespoons prepared yellow mustard
2   tablespoons ketchup (store-bought or homemade, pages 238-40)
1   teaspoon salt
⅓   cup cider vinegar

Combine the corn, onions, celery, red pepper, and pickle relish in a large, nonreactive bowl.

Combine the sugar, arrowroot or cornstarch, mustard, ketchup, and salt in a nonreactive saucepan, and mix well. Blend in the vinegar, until it is well incorporated. Cook over medium heat, stirring, until the sauce thickens. Pour the sauce over the corn mixture, tossing to coat evenly. Cover, and refrigerate for 1 hour.

This relish will keep for several days in the refrigerator.

■ **How to Use It:** Serve chilled or at room temperature with hot dogs, pork burgers, hamburgers, or any picnic meat.

Corn and Bean Salsa

This salsa, or relish, is substantial enough to call a side dish.

Makes about 5 cups

1   16-ounce can black beans, rinsed and drained
1   9-ounce package frozen corn kernels, thawed and drained
1   cup chopped ripe tomatoes
½   cup diced white onions
¼   cup minced green onions, white and green parts
¼   cup balsamic vinegar
2   tablespoons minced fresh parsley
1   tablespoon minced fresh cilantro
1   tablespoon Louisiana-style hot
     sauce
2   garlic cloves, pressed
1   teaspoon chili powder
1   teaspoon sea salt
1   whole dried chile pepper, crushed
½   teaspoon black pepper
½   teaspoon ground cumin
⅓   cup vegetable oil

Combine the beans, corn, tomatoes, and onions in a large, non-reactive bowl. Set aside.

In another bowl, combine the vinegar, parsley, cilantro, hot sauce, garlic, chili powder, salt, chile pepper, black pepper, and cumin. With a wire whisk, beat in the oil a little at a time, until the mixture is emulsified. Pour over the bean and corn mixture, and toss to mix well. Cover, and let sit in the refrigerator for several hours before serving.

This mixture will keep for several days in the refrigerator.

■ **How to Use It:** Serve at room temperature or chilled on grilled pork steak or on slices of barbecued pork shoulder.

Wild Mushroom Salsa

Just about any condiment or dipping sauce gets called a salsa today, so I call this mushroom sauce a salsa. You can call it whatever you want.

Makes about 3 cups

1   cup dried porcini mushrooms
1   cup boiling water
⅓   cup olive oil
½   cup minced red onions
1   tablespoon pressed garlic
2   teaspoons seeded and minced jalapeño
2   cups sliced fresh shiitake mushrooms (discard stems)
½   cup sliced white button mushrooms
½   cup diced red bell pepper
¼   cup dry vermouth
¼   cup fresh lime juice
2   tablespoons minced fresh parsley
1   tablespoon minced fresh cilantro
1   teaspoon crushed red pepper
1   teaspoon black pepper
1   teaspoon salt

Put the porcini mushrooms in a nonreactive bowl. Pour the boiling water over the mushrooms. Cover, and set aside for 20 minutes. Drain the porcinis, reserving any liquid, and chop them.

Heat the olive oil in a large, nonreactive saucepan over medium heat. Add the onions, garlic, and jalapeño, and sauté for 2 minutes. Add the rest of the ingredients, including the porcinis and any reserved liquid, and bring to a boil, stirring constantly. Reduce the heat, and simmer for 5 minutes. Serve hot.

This salsa will keep for 2 to 3 days in the refrigerator.

■ **How to Use It:** This salsa is excellent with steak.

Minted Honey Fig Relish

This relish is a very pleasant accompaniment to spicy food, especially lamb. It has a great flavor. It's also gooey, and thick, with a little bit of a crunch.

Makes about 2 1/2 cups

- ½ cup clover honey
- ¼ cup minced fresh mint
- ¼ cup red wine vinegar
- 2   cups diced fresh figs or 2 cups dried figs*
- 1   teaspoon sea salt

Pour the honey into a nonstick skillet, heating it until it foams. Stir in the rest of the ingredients, and blend well. Remove from the heat, and cool.

Serve at room temperature. This will keep for several weeks in the refrigerator.

■ How To Use It: This recipe is great with spicy lamb or chicken.

*Note: If you are using dried figs, soak them in warm water for 30 minutes, then dice them.

Jalapeño Chutney

This chutney offers sweetness and heat. The sweeter the mango chutney you put in it, the sweeter this chutney. If you are a fan of steak sauce, this chutney will hit the spot.

Makes about 3 cups

1   large red onion, peeled
5 to 6 jalapeños
¼   cup olive oil
2   cups prepared mango chutney
¼   cup minced fresh parsley
2   tablespoons minced fresh cilantro
4   garlic cloves, minced
2   tablespoons fresh lime juice
1   tablespoon light brown sugar
1   teaspoon salt

Preheat the oven to 350°F. Coat the onion and jalapeños with the olive oil. Roast until the onion is tender and the skins bubble on the peppers, 30 to 45 minutes.

Meanwhile, briefly process the chutney in a blender or in a food processor fitted with a steel blade until it is a finely chopped consistency.

Peel and seed the peppers (wear rubber gloves for this). Dice the peppers and onion. Place the peppers and onion and the chutney in a nonreactive bowl. Add all the remaining ingredients, and blend well. Refrigerate the chutney for 2 to 3 hours to let the flavors blend.

This chutney will keep for 1 week in the refrigerator.

■ **How to Use It:** Bring the chutney to room temperature before serving with grilled steak, chicken breast, or lamb chops.

■ **Variation:** An interesting change to this recipe is to grill or smoke the onion and peppers.

A Brief Lesson in Cutting Terms

Since we are using a lot of different products that are chopped, diced, minced, julienned, and everything in between, here are some useful definitions.

chop *v.* To cut into small pieces. Or, to cut into fairly regular pieces. The dimensions can vary according to the overall cooking time required: the longer the cooking time, the larger the pieces.

dice *v.* To cut into small cubes.

medium dice *n.* A neat cut in which pieces are quite regular, about 1/3 inch on each side.

large dice *n.* A neat cut in which pieces are quite regular, about 1/2 to 3/4 inch on each side.

mince *v.* To chop into fine, regular pieces. Or, to cut or chop into very small pieces.

julienne *adj.* Cut into long, thin strips (of vegetables) that measure about 1/8 inch square and 1 to 2 inches long.

purée *v.* To chop extremely fine.

Grilled Ratatouille Salsa

South of France, meet barbecue. Ratatouille is a traditional French dish made from eggplant, tomatoes, and summer squash. It's usually served as a side dish, but it also makes a fine topping for any grilled meat, especially since the vegetables in the ratatouille are also grilled.

Makes about 4 cups

1   medium eggplant, peeled
1   medium zucchini
1   medium yellow squash
¼   cup Italian Salad Dressing Marinade (page 90)
4   ripe plum tomatoes, chopped
½   cup oil-cured olives, pitted

HERBED DRESSING:
½   cup extra-virgin olive oil
3   tablespoons Dijon-style mustard
3   tablespoons fresh lemon juice
2   tablespoons minced fresh basil leaves
2   tablespoons minced fresh parsley
1   tablespoon Worcestershire sauce
1   tablespoon capers, drained
3   garlic cloves, pressed
1   teaspoon sea salt

Cut the eggplant, zucchini, and squash lengthwise into ½-inch-thick slices. Brush the vegetables with the marinade. Grill the vegetables over hot coals for about 5 minutes, or until the vegetables are tender, turning often.

Cut the vegetables into large dice. Combine in a bowl with tomatoes and olives.

Combine the Herbed Dressing ingredients in a small bowl. Mix well. Pour the dressing over the vegetables, and toss to coat evenly.

This salsa will keep for 2 to 3 days in the refrigerator.

■ **How to Use It:** Serve this warm or cold, as a side dish or a topping for any grilled meat.

■ **Variations:** You can use a different marinade to coat the vegetables, such as Basic Herbed Marinade (page 89), Chef Gary's Italian Marinade (page 92), or Shortcut Herbed Marinade (page 94).

■ Ketchup ■

Another must-have barbecue accompaniment is ketchup, and homemade ketchup makes great barbecue even better.

ketchup, also **catchup** or **catsup** *n.* A condiment consisting of a thick, smooth-textured, spicy sauce usually made from tomatoes.

Believe it or not, ketchup started out as a spicy pickled fish sauce that British seamen brought home to England in the 1700s. The Brits started making ketchup with grapes, nuts, mushrooms, cucumbers, and just about any fruit or vegetable they could lay their hands on. But when ketchup crossed the sea to America, New Englanders began making it with tomatoes, which is generally how it's made today—although you can find just about any sort of condiment labeled "ketchup" at a fancy food store, the same way that any relish can be called a salsa.

Ketchup is simple to make, it's delicious, and you can control the ingredients in it (salt, for instance). Ketchup usually has vinegar in it to give it tang and a sweetener of some sort to balance out the vinegar.

Easy Homemade Ketchup

Step aside, store-bought ketchup! You may never go back to the bottled kind once you've tasted ketchup you've made fresh at home.

Makes about 1 cup

1   6-ounce can tomato paste
¼   cup brown sugar, packed
3   tablespoons cider vinegar
3   tablespoons water or stock
¼   teaspoon dry mustard powder
¼   teaspoon ground cinnamon
¼   teaspoon salt
⅛   teaspoon ground cloves
⅛   teaspoon ground allspice

Americans spend more than $23 billion annually on fresh beef.

Combine all of the ingredients in a nonreactive bowl, and blend well. Store in an airtight container in the refrigerator for up to 1 month.

You can also mix the ingredients in a saucepan and then heat the mixture, letting it simmer for about 30 minutes. I like this method better because the spices infuse more thoroughly with the help of the heat, resulting in a slightly better ketchup.

■ **How to Use It:** Use this any way you would use store-bought ketchup.

Traditional Homemade Ketchup

In this recipe you can adjust the amounts of brown sugar and vinegar to get the sweet-sour balance you like. You can also add more garlic, mustard, or cayenne for more heat.

Makes about 8 cups

- 4 cups tomato paste
- 3 cups white vinegar
- 1⅔ cups brown sugar, packed
- 2 cups water
- 2 teaspoons granulated garlic
- 2 teaspoons ground cinnamon
- 2 teaspoons dry mustard powder
- 2 teaspoons seasoned salt
- 1 teaspoon ground coriander
- 1 teaspoon cayenne
- ½ teaspoon ground cloves
- ¼ teaspoon ground nutmeg

Combine all of the ingredients in a nonreactive saucepan and place over medium heat. Bring the mixture to a boil, stirring constantly. Reduce the heat and simmer for 30 minutes, stirring occasionally. Cool, then bottle and store in the refrigerator for up to 1 month.

■ **How to Use It:** Use this any way you would use store-bought ketchup.

Spicy Tomato Ketchup

Because of the demand for hotter foods, several manufacturers are just coming out with spicy varieties of ketchup. You can be ahead of the times with your own spicy ketchup.

Makes about 5 pints

10 pounds ripe tomatoes, coarsely chopped
2 cups chopped onions
½ cup chopped red bell pepper
1 tablespoon dry mustard powder
1 tablespoon black pepper
1 tablespoon sea salt
2 teaspoons dried basil
2 teaspoons ground coriander
1 teaspoon allspice
1 teaspoon cayenne
1 teaspoon ground cinnamon
½ teaspoon powdered bay leaf
2 cups brown sugar, packed
1½ cups cider vinegar

Combine the tomatoes, onions, and red pepper in a bowl. Process in a blender or food processor with a steel blade, until puréed. Press through a wire strainer or chinois, and discard the pulp. You should have about 6 quarts of purée.

In a very large nonreactive saucepan, bring the purée to a boil over medium-high heat. Reduce the heat, and simmer, uncovered, stirring often, until the purée is reduced by half, about an hour.

Add the mustard, pepper, salt, basil, coriander, allspice, cayenne, cinnamon, and bay leaf. Stir vigorously to blend. Simmer for 30 minutes. Blend in the brown sugar, and continue cooking over medium heat until very thick (another 1½ to 2 hours). As the mixture thickens, reduce the heat, and stir often to prevent sticking and scorching. Blend in the vinegar during the last 15 minutes of the cooking process.

Pour the ketchup into pint jars. The ketchup stores well in the refrigerator for 3 to 4 weeks.

■ **How to Use It:** Any way you would use store-bought ketchup.

Volume and Fluid Weight Equivalents

1 tablespoon	=	½ fluid ounce	=	3 teaspoons		
2 tablespoons	=	1 fluid ounce	=	⅛ cup		
4 tablespoons	=	2 fluid ounces	=	¼ cup		
8 tablespoons	=	4 fluid ounces	=	½ cup		
16 tablespoons	=	8 fluid ounces	=	1 cup	=	½ pint
2 cups	=	16 fluid ounces	=	1 pint		
4 cups	=	32 fluid ounces	=	2 pints	=	1 quart
16 cups	=	128 fluid ounces	=	4 quarts	=	1 gallon

Quantity Guide for Rubs,
Marinades, Mops, and Sauces

This chart provides you with the approximate quantities of rub,
marinade, mop, or sauce you will need to prepare different types
of meat. Use it to decide whether to double or triple a recipe for
the cut of meat you've chosen. Or use it to figure out how much
marinade or baste you want to set aside for a later use, before it
has come in contact with uncooked meat.

Type of Meat	Quantity	Amount of Rub
Whole chicken	3 to 4 pounds	¼ cup
Whole turkey	12 pounds	½ cup
Pork ribs	3 to 4 pounds	¼ cup
Pork shoulder or butt	3 to 5 pounds	¼ cup
Pork loin	3 to 5 pounds	¼ cup
Pork tenderloin	1 to 2 pounds	2 tblspns
Whole beef brisket	7 to 12 pounds	¾ to 1 cup
Brisket flat	3 to 5 pounds	¼ cup
Strip steak	2 to 3 pounds	1 to 2 tblspns
Leg of lamb	6 to 8 pounds	¼ cup
Fish fillets	6 medium-size/ 3 pounds	¼ cup

Amount of Marinade	Amount of Mop/Sop/Baste	Amount of Sauce
1 cup	¼ cup	¼ cup
2 cups	½ cup	1 cup
2 cups	½ cup	¼ cup
1 cup	½ cup	¼ cup
1 cup	½ cup	¼ cup
½ cup	¼ cup	¼ cup
3 cups	1 cup	1 cup
1 cup	½ cup	½ cup
½ cup	¼ cup	¼ cup
1 cup	½ cup	½ cup
2 cups	½ cup	½ cup

Resources

Spices and Seasonings

The following is a list of companies that have helped and worked with me over the years. Their products are fresh and grade A. They also ship almost anywhere, and most will do custom spice blending.

Ingredients Corporation of America
676 Huron Avenue
Memphis, Tennessee 38107
Phone: 901-525-4422
Fax: 901-525-4425

Mo Hotta Mo Betta
P. O. Box 4136
San Luis Obispo, California 93403
Phone: 800-462-3220
Fax: 800-618-4454

Pendery's
1221 Manufacturing
Dallas, Texas 75207
Phone: 800-533-1870
Fax: 214-761-1966

Oregon Spice Company
1630 Southeast Rhine Street
Portland, Oregon 97202
Phone: 503-238-0664
Fax: 503-238-3872

Penzeys, Ltd.
P. O. Box 933
Muskego, Wisconsin 53150

Phone: 414-679-7207
Fax: 414-679-7878

The Pepper Gal
P. O. Box 23006
Ft. Lauderdale, Florida 33307
Phone: 954-537-5540
Fax: 954-566-2208

Pisciotta's Produce Co.
217 East Missouri Avenue
Kansas City, Missouri 64106
Phone: 816-221-6670
Fax: 816-842-1559

The Planters Seed & Spice Co.
513 Walnut Street
Kansas City, Missouri 64106
Phone: 816-842-3651
Fax: 816-842-1422

Spices, Etc.
P. O. Box 5266
Charlottesville, Virginia 22905
Phone: 800-827-6373
Fax: 800-827-0145

Vann's Spices Ltd.
1238 East Joppa Road
Baltimore, Maryland 21286
Phone: 410-583-1643 or 800-583-1693
Fax: 410-583-1783

Barbecue Sauces and Bottling

BBQ Sauce of the Month Club and
Boarbroom Bar-B-Q
9600 Antioch
Overland Park, Kansas 66212
Phone: 913-642-6273 or 800-873-0710
Fax: 913-642-2469

Porky's Gourmet Foods
P. O. Box 830
Ridgetop, Tennessee 37152
Phone: 800-PORK911 (800-767-5911)
Fax: 615-244-RIBS (615-244-7427)

Vanity Bottling
Micro-Bottling—Your Sauce or Our Sauce
3625 West 50th Terrace
Shawnee Mission, Kansas 66205

Source for Whole Hogs

Although I don't really address cooking a whole hog in this book, I am often asked where one can get a whole hog to cook for a party. W & G has outlets all over the country. In addition, they ship orders of anywhere from 1 to 1,000 government-inspected hogs, all around the United States.

W & G Marketing Co., Inc.
Executive Office Building
413 Kellogg Avenue
Ames, Iowa 50010
Phone: 515-233-4050
Fax: 515-233-6229

Barbecue Pits, Smokers, and Grills

What is the best barbecue pit? My answer is, any pit whose temperature you can *learn* how to control. There are a lot of good barbecue pits out there, and if you think you may have found one, see if you can make arrangements to cook on it before purchasing it, or get referrals from people who have used the same model. I am only going to suggest one pit, because at this writing it is the main pit I am using. It's a trailer-style pit that David Klose and I designed, with help from friends.

Bar-B-Que Pits by Klose
2214½ West 34th Street
Houston, Texas 77018
Phone: 800-487-7487
Fax: 713-686-8793

When I'm doing hamburgers, sausages, or steaks for a big crowd, or when I want to barbecue a whole hog on a spit, I like to use my Big John Grill & Rotisserie. It's well built and it's easy to use.

Big John Grills and Rotisseries
West College Avenue
P. O. Box 5250
Pleasant Gap, Pennsylvania 16823
Phone: 800-326-9575 or 814-359-2755
Fax: 814-359-2621

In addition to the items I mentioned above, I use the Kingsford Pro-Grill, a Weber kettle grill (22½"), and the Weber Smoky Mountain Cooker smoker. I have also been using and demonstrating gas grills from Phoenix Grill Co. and by Superb Cooking Products, Empire Comfort Systems, Inc. Other products I recommend are Charwood smoker oven grills and the Masa Grill from Baykal & Company.

Following are a list of the companies which manufacture these products, as well as many other pits, smokers, and grills. Call for catalogs or retail locations.

Masa Grill
Baykal & Company
P. O. Box 5005
Rancho Santa Fe, California 92067
Phone: 800-793-7035
Fax: 619-793-4506

Big Green Egg
3414 Clairmont Road
Atlanta, Georgia 30319
Phone: 800-939-EGGS (800-939-3447)
Fax: 404-321-0330

The Brinkmann Corporation
4215 McEwen Road
Dallas, Texas 75244
Phone: 800-468-5252

Broilmaster
Martin Industries
P. O. Box 128
Florence, Alabama 35631
Phone: 800-277-1055
Fax: 205-740-5192

Char-Broil Grill Lover's Catalog
P. O. Box 1300
Columbus, Georgia 31902
Phone: 800-241-8981
Fax: 706-571-7029

Charwood
Division of Custom Firescreen
108 Jefferson Avenue
Des Moines, Iowa 50314
Phone: 800-284-1517
Fax: 515-243-3915

Cookshack, Inc.
2304 North Ash Street
Ponca City, Oklahoma 74601
Phone: 800-423-0698

Hasty-Bake, Inc.
7656 East 46th Street
Tulsa, Oklahoma 74145
Phone: 800-4AN-OVEN (800-426-6836)
Fax: 918-665-8225

Jedmaster Cookers
Jedco, Inc.
2773 Frontier Road
Canton, Kansas 67428
Phone: 888-227-2283

Kingsford Charcoal Grills
Porcelain Metals, Inc.
1400 South 13th Street
Louisville, Kentucky 40210
Phone: 800-585-4745

MHP—Modern Home Products
150 South Ram Road
Antioch, Illinois 60002
Phone: 888-647-4745
Fax: 847-395-9121

New Braunfels Smoker Co.
P. O. Box 310698
New Braunfels, Texas 78130
Phone: 800-232-3398
Fax: 210-629-9140

Oklahoma Joe's
1616 West Airport Road
Stillwater, Oklahoma 74075
Phone: 800-227-JOES (800-227-5637)
Fax: 405-377-3083

Phoenix Grill Co.
P. O. Box 250
Sanford, North Carolina 27331
Phone: 800-438-3348
Fax: 919-776-0121

Pitt's & Spitt's
14221 Eastex Freeway
Houston, Texas 77032
Phone: 800-521-2947
Fax: 713-442-4252

Sunbeam Hot-Off-the-Grill Catalog
Sunbeam Consumer Affairs
P. O. Box 948389
Maitland, Florida 32794
Phone: 800-621-6929

Superb Cooking Products
Empire Comfort Systems, Inc.
918 Freeburg Avenue
Belleville, Illinois 62222
Phone: 800-851-3153 or 618-233-7420
Fax: 800-443-8648

Traeger Industries
Box 829
1385 East College Street
Mount Angel, Oregon 97036
Phone: 800-872-3437

Weber-Stephen Products
250 South Hicks Road
Palatine, Illinois 60067
Phone: 800-446-1071 or, for answers to grilling questions
    April 1–Labor Day, the Grilling Hotline,
    800-GRILL-OUT (800-474-5568)

Barbecue Societies and Publications

Big Apple BBQ Association
c/o Richard "Smoky" Alexander, director
7 East 14th Street, Suite 919
New York, New York 10003
Phone: 212-989-0021
Fax: 212-727-3808
email: alexande@interport.net

California BBQ Association (CBBQA)
c/o Frank Boyer
21911 Bear Creek Way
Los Gatos, California 95033
Phone: 408-354-4693 or 408-354-1237
email: frankbbq@ix.netcom.com
This association's newsletter is published six times a year.

Greater Omaha Barbecue Society (GOBS)
4928 North 105th Street
Omaha, Nebraska 68134
Phone: 402-493-1474
Membership is $20 per year, includes subscription
    to *The Drippings* monthly newsletter.

Greater Wichita Barbecue Society
2135 North Riverside Boulevard
Wichita, Kansas 67203
316-264-5115

International BBQ Cookers Association (IBCA)
P. O. Box 300556
Arlington, Texas 76007
Phone: 817-469-1579
Send $20 for a one-year membership, and an
additional $20 to receive a promoter's pack.

Kansas City Barbeque Society (KCBS)
11514 Hickman Mills Drive
Kansas City, MO 64134
Phone: 816-765-5891 or 800-963-KCBS (800-963-5227)
Membership is $30 per year, and includes subscription
to monthly newsletter *KC Bullsheet.*

Lone Star Barbecue Society (LSBS)
P. O. Box 120771
Arlington, Texas 76012
Phone: 817-795-9507
Fax: 817-795-1968
Membership is $20 per year, and $5 to include a spouse.
Subscription to newsletter is part of membership.

National Barbecue Association (NBBQA)
c/o Theresa Salmen
4425 Randolph Road, Suite 304
Charlotte, North Carolina 28211
Phone: 704-365-3622
Fax: 704-365-3678
Annual membership $35 for individual or $125 for
business. Membership includes a subscription to
monthly newsletter. Holds an annual conference
and trade show.

National Barbecue News
c/o Joe Phelps or Don Gillis
P. O. Box 981
Douglas, Georgia 31533
Phone: 912-384-0001
Fax: 912-384-4220
Send $18 for a one-year subscription to monthly
barbecue newsletter.

New England Barbecue Society (NEBS)
P. O. Box 97
North Billerica, Massachusetts 01862
Membership is $25 annually.

Pacific Northwest Barbecue Association (PNWBA)
c/o Bob Lyon
4244 134th Avenue SE
Bellevue, Washington 98006
Phone: 206-643-0607
Send $10 for four issues of *Drippings from the Pit.*

The Pits
c/o Susan Tindall
7714 Hillard
Dallas, Texas 75217
Phone: 214-398-4374
Send $20 for a one-year/ten issue subscription.

USA Smoke Barbecue News
c/o Jennifer Bates
Route 2, Box 73B
Hico, Texas 76457
Phone: 254-785-2212
Fax: 254-785-2213
Send $22 for a one-year/twelve issue subscription
    ($36 outside the U.S.).

Product Development

If you want help developing a unique barbecue sauce, steak
sauce, rub, or seasoning, these companies can help you.

Jason Foods & Old Mill Foods
BBQMASON™
P. O. Box 605
Elk Horn, Nebraska 68022
Phone: 402-779-2403
Fax: 402-779-4057

Kansas City Baron of Barbecue™ Products Co.
3625 West 50th Terrace
Shawnee Mission, Kansas 66205

Barbecue Classes, Tapes, and Videos

Barbecue videos by Paul Kirk address barbecuing, from backyard
to competition. The videos include:

Volume I: Barbecued ribs, chicken, and basic rubs.
Volume II: Barbecued brisket, pork butt, and
basic barbecue sauce.
Volume III: Whole hog, salmon, lamb, advanced rub
and barbecue sauce.

The videos are available from:

K.C. Specialties
P. O. Box 8293
Shawnee Mission, Kansas 66208
Phone: 913-384-7367
Fax: 913-262-2174
email: 76703.551@compuserve.com

If you are interested in taking a School of Pitmasters class from
Paul Kirk, you can reach him through the Kansas City Barbeque
Society, phone 816-765-5891.

Index